Penguin Books

Self-Help

Morris Gleitzman was born in England and moved to Australia as a teenager. After brief careers in the television and yuletide industries, he became a children's author and newspaper columnist. He hopes readers won't define him solely by the 57 personal failings listed in this book, as there are heaps more he couldn't fit in. For some of them, and details of all his other books, visit Morris at his website: www.morrisgleitzman.com

Also by Morris Gleitzman

MORRIS GLEITZMAN

Self Help Less

57 PIECES OF CRUCIAL ADVICE FOR PEOPLE WHO NEED A BIT MORE TIME TO GET IT RIGHT

To Michael,
Bonnie and
the wonderful
I Clusion team.
You don't need any
more time to get
it right!
Thanks,
Mo...

Penguin Books

Penguin Books Australia Ltd
487 Maroondah Highway, PO Box 257
Ringwood, Victoria 3134, Australia
Penguin Books Ltd
Harmondsworth, Middlesex, England
Penguin Putnam Inc.
375 Hudson Street, New York, New York 10014, USA
Penguin Books Canada Limited
10 Alcorn Avenue, Toronto, Ontario, Canada M4V 3B2
Penguin Books (NZ) Ltd
Cnr Rosedale and Airborne Roads, Albany, Auckland, New Zealand
Penguin Books (South Africa) (Pty) Ltd
5 Watkins Street, Denver Ext. 4, 2094, South Africa
Penguin Books India (P) Ltd
11, Community Centre, Panchsheel Park, New Delhi 110 017, India

This collection first published by Penguin Books Australia Ltd 2000

1 3 5 7 9 10 8 6 4 2

Design by Tony Palmer and Adrian Saunders, Penguin Design Studio

Typeset in 10.5/14 Sabon by Midland Typesetters, Maryborough, Victoria
Made and printed in Australia by Australian Print Group, Maryborough, Victoria

National Library of Australia Cataloguing-in-Publication data:

Gleitzman, Morris, 1953– .
Self-helpless: 57 pieces of crucial advice for people who
need a bit more time to get it right.

ISBN 0 14 029256 X.

1. Self-help techniques – Anecdotes. 2. Self-help
techniques – Humor. I. Title. II. Title: Fifty-seven
pieces of crucial advice for people who need a bit more
time to get it right.

A828.302

www.penguin.com.au

For
Aurora Hammond
and
Peter O'Connor

CONTENTS

INTRODUCTION

WHEN I WAS a kid I read a lot of science-fiction comics. I think it was the boundless possibilities of space that attracted me, and the way the space-suits were designed to reveal cleavage, even on the women.

I used to read them in bed. Then, after lights out, I'd toss and turn in the grip of lustful fantasies. Not about the cleavage, about the boundless possibilities of the cosmos.

I'd fantasise about other worlds where true human happiness was possible, even for skinny kids with an underbite who were no good at maths. I'd dream of planets where maths teachers weren't allowed to twist boys' ears, not even to demonstrate the geometric properties of irregular shapes. I'd conjure up meteorite clusters inhabited by orthodontists who'd never heard of wire and sharp plastic and who preferred to work in marshmallow. I'd invent entire solar systems where kids who laughed at other kids' upper arms got eaten by stick insects.

The years passed, and human space exploration fell sadly short of what I was counting on for happiness in adult life. Desperate, I sent science-fiction comics to the presidents of the US and the USSR. Well, I tried to, but the newsagent said he didn't deliver past Cosgrove Street.

Then, as I moved through my teens, I found I was spending less and less time gazing up at the stars and trying to calculate how many soda-syphon bulbs I'd need to achieve lift-off. I started reading things that weren't science-fiction comics or Gestetner-duplicated pamphlets claiming that aliens were already among us but had been jailed for shoplifting.

I started reading self-help books. Not self-help books as we know them today, because in the late sixties, despite a global explosion of social and spiritual alternative-seeking, there were no sections in bookshops called Self-Help. Very few books actually described themselves as such, and those that did were mostly about setting up goat-farming communes or building meditation stools out of kelp.

For me, though, almost every book I read was a self-help book. *Of Human Bondage* by Somerset Maugham. *Tender Is The Night* by F. Scott Fitzgerald. *The Electric Kool-Aid Acid Test* by Tom Wolfe. And swags of stuff by such self-help gurus as Wordsworth, Nabokov, Orwell, Aristotle, Lawrence, Shakespeare, Joyce,

Christina Stead, Hal Porter, George Johnston and C. J. Dennis.

I realised, belatedly and with their guidance, that the most crucial and challenging human exploration takes place not in some distant galaxy among giant four-dimensional stick insects with Gestetner fluid for blood, but in a much weirder and scarier place – inside ourselves.

There's an old saying in the storytelling trade: 'Show, don't tell.' That's what the great self-help writers have done over the centuries. They've shown us our touching dopey selves in such a way that we absorb great truths and big questions and precious droplets of understanding without once seeing the word 'self-actualisation'.

Today it's different. You could land a 96-seater spaceship on the Self-Help shelves in most bookshops and still have room for free-range goat-farming up the other end. There are thousands and thousands of purpose-written self-help books, many with titles in the imperative. *Feel the Fear And Do It Anyway. Buy This Book And Then Buy My Next One.* And most of them preferring to tell rather than show.

Please don't get me wrong. Some of them do it brilliantly. Some of them have changed my life just as much as any nineteenth-century Russian novel rich in poetic sub-text and symbolic peasants with allegorical skin complaints. Modern self-help books are rarely poetic, but often superbly efficient. They communicate not by osmosis, but by direct injection into the frontal lobes. Which is exactly what we busy folk need when we can't take long holidays and have to make our inner journeys weekend getaways.

Superbly efficient, these modern self-help books, but

just a bit terrifying. They define our goals so absolutely, and our shortcomings, and the yawning gulf between. They're fantastically useful, these bold and assertive Baedeckers of the inner life, but there is one little drawback. Somehow this vast inner peace-keeping force, who are far too efficient to ever mix a metaphor like I've just done, dedicated as they are to the creation of human happiness through the banishment of anxiety, make us feel horribly anxious.

Which is where this book comes in.

For ten years I wrote a regular semi-autobiographical newspaper column. I say semi-autobiographical because, while each column was based on an incident, theme, habit, thought, peccadillo, experience and/or mishap from my life, each one was injected with a large squirt of comic exaggeration. It's what you do when you're trying to be honest about your life and you want your family to sit at the same table as you in restaurants. And at home.

Last year I decided to treat myself to a year or two off from the column, partly to concentrate on a couple of tricky kids' books I wanted to write, and partly because I was hoping the pets would come to accept food from me again. One night, sick of being snubbed by goldfish, I took refuge in my armchair and started reading back through my columns, searching for incidents that could have so hurt the feelings of two young marine vertebrates.

I was horrified by what I read. Not only had I shamelessly exposed the private lives of Jaws and Willy to public scrutiny, I'd done even worse to myself. As I read back through six years of columns, which was as far as I could bring myself to go, I saw they revealed a litany of personal shortcomings. They exposed me as a walking encyclopaedia of human failings. Me, who'd been reading self-help books for thirty years and was quietly confident that my failings were now largely restricted to scalp-related issues.

I panicked. I rushed to a large bookstore, intending to buy everything on the Self-Help shelf. I'd have needed a semi to get them home, but I didn't care. I obviously hadn't read enough self-help books in my life, or I hadn't read them properly, and I wasn't going to make the same mistake the second time around. 'Imbecile,' I muttered to myself as I lugged the first armload to the counter. 'Cretin. Careless and inadequate reader of self-help books.'

Then, inside me, I heard a tiny voice piping up amidst the self-loathing and hurtful name-calling. I'm still not sure exactly whose voice it was. Wordsworth, possibly, or Nabokov, or maybe even C. J. Dennis. 'Don't be so hard on yourself, you dopey bugger,' said the voice. 'It takes ages to get it right. What are you, some sort of frustrated maths teacher? Be kind to yourself.'

My eyes filled with tears and I put the books back on the shelf, all except the ones with chapters on apologising to pets. The voice was right. How can we ever hope to help ourselves, with or without the aid of books, if we're always calling ourselves names and booting ourselves up the bum?

It's with that thought that I offer you this volume. If, like me, you need a bit more time to get it right, I hope reading this book will encourage you to be kinder to yourself along the way. If it doesn't, I hope at least you'll get some solace and enjoyment from the spectacle of someone else consistently getting it wrong.

ADDICTION

Every form of addiction is bad, no matter whether the narcotic be alcohol or morphine or idealism.

C. G. Jung

I wonder if that's a bit harsh? True, some people suffer terribly from their addictions, and cause others to suffer too, and I'd support anything that reduces human suffering as long as it doesn't involve putting shampoo up rabbits' noses. But what if things are a bit different for most of us? What if our addictions don't cause us or anyone else actual suffering, just occasional loss of dignity (us) and exasperation (them)? Call me an idealist, but what if our addictions bring us much-needed moments of pleasure and muscular relief as we grapple with all our other dysfunctions? OK, all my other dysfunctions.

IT WAS LATE, very late, but I could have made it. I could have tiptoed from the front door to my bedroom without waking the kids if it hadn't been for all the things cluttering up the hallway. The vacuum cleaner. The Lego pirate ship. The social worker.

I didn't see the social worker at first. Not until I'd stepped on the vacuum cleaner and somersaulted and removed the rigging from the pirate ship with my front teeth and she'd switched on the light. I lay on the hall carpet, blinking up at all the faces. The social worker. The kids. The plastic pirates on the lower deck. They all looked disapproving and a little sad.

'Dad,' said the kids quietly, 'we know about your problem.'

My head spun. How had they discovered my guilty secret? I decided to deny everything. 'Problem?' I said. 'What problem?'

The kids rolled their eyes. The social worker sighed. The plastic pirates didn't do anything but I could tell they didn't believe me either.

'Your tragic inability to stay away from bars,' said the kids. 'Especially fruit and nut.'

'It's not true,' I shouted. 'I've given up chocolate. I haven't had any chocolate in months.'

The kids sighed. 'What's that brown stuff around your mouth?' they said.

'Gunpowder,' I said. 'From the pirate ship.'

The kids sighed again. 'Dad,' they said, 'we know you've been to the 24-hour shop at the service station.'

I staggered to my feet. 'The car needed new brake linings,' I protested. Several bars of chocolate slipped out of my shirt and thudded to the floor. The kids looked at me sadly.

'The shop was out of brake linings,' I said, 'but they

reckoned family-size blocks of Dairy Milk would do the job just as well.'

The social worker patted my arm. 'Admitting you've got a problem is the first stage of recovery,' she said.

'Look,' I pleaded. 'I like a bit of chocolate every now and then, what's the problem with that? Napoleon marched his troops to Russia on chocolate.'

The kids held up a familiar-looking soggy brown object. 'Yes,' they said, 'but when he ran out, he didn't get desperate and try to extract his own by boiling Milo up in a sock.'

I grimaced at the memory. It had been almost as unsuccessful as stirring sugar into Vegemite.

'OK,' I said. 'I am a little bit addicted to chocolate. But what's so bad about that? Everybody's got at least one tiny area of compulsive behaviour in their lives. It's normal, right?'

The kids pointed to the remains of the dinner I'd made that night.

'People have cooked with chocolate for centuries,' I protested.

'Not curries,' said the kids.

That's when I broke down. 'You're right,' I sobbed. 'I do have a problem and I want to be cured.'

The Centre for Socially Approved Addictions was an anonymous brick building tucked away in a quiet suburb. A friendly nurse showed me to my ward. 'Lights out at 11,' she said, 'and no caddies in the room.'

I stared at her uncomprehendingly.

She looked at her clipboard. 'Sorry,' she said, 'you're

in for chocolate. I thought you were in for something else.'

The penny dropped. 'Golf,' I said.

'No,' she said, 'tea.'

I wandered down to the canteen. The other patients seemed a friendly lot too.

'You'd be, you know, amazed,' said one man, 'how many different, you know, addictions and compulsive habits are being treated under this one, you know, roof.'

A woman at the same table checked her lipstick in her compact mirror and nodded in agreement.

'It's incredible,' she said, checking her lipstick again. 'Half of us here didn't even know we had problems.' She paused to check her lipstick.

'How did you discover yours?' I asked.

'Watching *The Crying Game* on video,' she said, peering into her mirror. 'I'd sat through it 11 times and I still hadn't spotted the woman was a bloke.'

That night there was a distressing incident. A patient in for lawn-mowing had smuggled a Victa two-stroke in with his pyjamas and was caught mowing his bedroom carpet. As he was being wheeled away by two burly nurses, another patient in for car-cleaning flung himself at the trolley in an attempt to wipe it down with a chamois and was almost run over. I was glad I was in the comparative safety of the Chocolate Wing with its distinctive brown wallpaper. There were no incidents there, mostly because we were all too busy licking the walls.

The next morning, though, things turned ugly again. We all had to visit the doctor, except the people who were addicted to visiting the doctor. They had to do the washing-up, which upset the people who were addicted to doing the washing-up.

As the building rang with the sounds of breaking crockery and cries of 'I'll just run these few things under the tap,' I decided to leave. I slipped out through a back door, right into the middle of an aversion therapy session for addicted golfers.

It's amazing. Since being hit in the head by that golf ball, I haven't had a single craving for chocolate. The kids are very relieved. I'm not becoming complacent, though, because I know few of us make it through life free of some sort of addictive behaviour. In fact, I must read a book on the subject. Just as soon as I've finished vacuuming my Lego pirate ship.

ANGER

Get stuffed.
Anonymous

*Could anger be the secret energy that fuels our passions,
neuroses, jokes and tumours? We're told to own it,
express it freely, but not allow it to damage ourselves,
others or the sovereignty of nations. No wonder it's
always looking for sneaky ways to get out. Fortunately
for us and our pets, life is full of small, defenceless,
completely stupid inanimate objects.*

CHRISTOPHER SKASE, I'm afraid I've said some angry
things about you over the years, particularly my
suggestion to the Federal Police that your oxygen
cylinders are actually very large cocktail shakers.

Margaret Thatcher, I'm sorry for that comment I made
in the butchers years ago comparing you to a stainless

steel offal compactor (the one that was roughly the same height as you).

Ronald Reagan, I should never have sent you that letter offering you a job at my place as a doorstop. (Though I must say I was flattered and charmed by your acceptance.)

To each of you my sincerest apologies, and the same to Colonel Gaddafi, General Pinochet and Madonna (or the woman who looks just like her who took my park at the supermarket), because I realise now it's not you I'm angry with, it's self-adhesive price tags.

This realisation came the other day as I was taking the self-adhesive price tag off a plastic salad drainer. Seconds after starting I felt unkind thoughts about King Olaf of Norway well up inside me. By the time the tag was off I was seething and ready to send him a very stiff fax about his treatment of Swedish border settlers. I'm being ridiculous, I thought. I know very little about the geo-politics of that part of Scandinavia, plus King Olaf died in 1003.

Then it hit me. It wasn't really King Olaf I was angry about, it was the self-adhesive price tag. I was stunned. I'd never given price tags a second thought. Price tags were just things you plucked off as soon as you got home so your partner couldn't see how much you'd blown on a plastic salad drainer.

Except, I now admitted, scraping away with my finger-nail and a screwdriver and a power sander, you very rarely get to pluck a self-adhesive price tag off. Grind, file, chisel, but not pluck. Whenever I've had to remove an adhesive price tag, pluck is not the word that's sprung to my lips.

'Plus,' I shouted at the kitchen utensils, 'most of them

leave a sticky patch that's impossible to get off even if you live in Hollywood and can get Joan Collins in from next door to have a go with her fingernails.'

The kitchen utensils remained silent. I could see they thought I was making a big fuss about nothing even though most of them were sporting sticky patches. I looked sadly at my new salad drainer with its new sticky patch that would soon have food particles adhering to it, and dishcloth fibres, and other salad drainers.

'Over-adhesive price tags might be nothing to you,' I said to the kitchen utensils, 'as mightn't petrol pumps that drip on your foot and milk cartons that don't open properly when you Squeeze Edges To Push Spout Out, but I'm as mad as Peter Finch in *Network* and I want to find out why these price tags are inappropriately adhered before I publicly insult another European head of State.'

I asked a retailer. She scratched her head with her pricing gun. For a horrible moment I thought she was going to give herself a sticky patch.

'Dunno,' she said, 'unless it's to stop customers switching price tags.' I thought about that. Once it might have been possible to buy a plastic salad drainer and go into a car showroom and switch the tags, but not now surely, not with bar codes and the absence of 60,000-kilometre warranties on salad drainers.

There had to be another answer and I decided the place to find it was a self-adhesive price tag factory. Or a good three-volume history of price tags, but I couldn't refer to mine as they were all stuck together on the bookshelf.

The price tag factory was hard to spot at first, being

overshadowed on one side by a milk carton factory and on the other by an oil refinery. The factory executives were easy to miss too, at least the ones that had office partitions stuck to them.

I flung my salad drainer at their feet. Or tried to, but it was glued to my fingers.

'Why?' I shouted at them with a fury I'd previously reserved for third-world despots (to whom I now also apologise).

The executives exchanged nervous smiles. 'It's working,' they whispered.

I was confused.

The managing director sat me down and explained. 'It's simple,' he said. 'For years we made price tags that came off easily and didn't leave a mark and nobody gave us a second thought. So we consulted the experts and they said the best way to get noticed is to make a nuisance of yourself.'

'They told us the same,' said the milk carton executives, who were over for afternoon tea. 'We were sick of people only being interested in the milk and ignoring the carton.'

'It was worse for us,' said the oil company executives, who were over for discussions about the possibility of putting self-adhesive price tags on petrol. 'People didn't even see our product until the experts told us to rig all our pumps to drip.'

The executives went back to their afternoon tea. While they were occupied trying to get the milk carton open, I had a quiet word with the managing director. 'These experts,' I said. 'Where did you find them?'

The MD rolled his eyes. 'Wasn't easy,' he said.

'Margaret Thatcher was writing her memoirs, Christopher Skase was overseas and Ronald Reagan had just accepted a job elsewhere. In the end we had to use General Pinochet and a woman who stole my park at the supermarket.'

ANXIETY

If you forget to take one dose, you should not make up for the missing dose by doubling the dose at the next dosing time.
Patient product information,
Valium

If we were charged for anxiety at the same rate as electricity and water, my bills would be huge, even at off-peak rates. In a typical day I'm anxious about several hundred things. And I know I'm not the only one, judging from the global consumption of meditation, yoga and diazepam. Unfortunately none of those remedies work for me, but I have managed to achieve one small breakthrough. I no longer feel so anxious about feeling anxious.

MY HEART was pounding as I walked into the bookshop. I waited until there were no other customers at the counter and sidled over. Nervously I handed the assistant a slip of paper and asked her to read it.

'Do you have a copy,' she read, 'of *Pronunciation Anxiety: A Self-Help Guide For Sufferers?*' I marvelled at her bravery. She hadn't even hesitated before pronouncing 'pronunciation'.

'Sorry,' she said, 'we haven't got it in stock but we can order it in for you if you can tell us the publisher.'

This was what I had dreaded. My heart started to thump. My stomach started to churn. The bookshop started to spin. 'Doesn't matter,' I blurted, 'I'll try Kmart.' Then everything went black.

I came to on a stretcher. 'Tragic,' I heard one of the ambulance officers say to the other. 'Poor bugger can't pronounce "Farrar, Straus and Giroux".'

'It's worse than that,' I sobbed, as they lifted me into the ambulance, 'I can't pronounce any of the major American publishers.'

The ambulance officers looked down at me, compassion creasing their faces. 'Don't despair, mate,' one of them said gently. 'My brother-in-law had that. Kept forgetting to say the "k" in "Knopf". They fixed him up with a mnemonic. He just had to keep repeating to himself "How the knell do you say Knopf?" Cured him overnight.'

'You don't understand,' I whispered. 'I can't even say "mnemonic".'

The doctors quickly recognised that my condition needed urgent treatment and I was admitted to a Pronunciation Anxiety Clinic. That afternoon I met my specialist, a white-haired man in his sixties with a kindly face and a name tag that filled me with terror. 'Hello, I'm Doctor Smythe,' he said cheerily, 'pronounced "Smith".' I fainted.

Before my treatment started, he gave me a thorough examination. 'No obvious physical malformations,' he said, 'though there are signs of a recent sprain in your lower jaw.'

I nodded, wincing at the memory. 'That would have been when I was discussing *The Piano*.' I said. 'There'd been a Harvey Keitel scare the week before. Someone on telly had put the stress on the "Keit" instead of the "el". Halfway through a sentence I panicked and the whole thing just locked.'

The specialist nodded gravely. 'We see a lot of that. We've got a ward here full of people who were holding dinner parties spellbound with brilliant reinterpretations of post-impressionism, then realised too late that the next artist they had to mention was Van Gogh.'

'You mean,' I said excitedly, 'I'm not alone in my affliction?'

The specialist shook his head. 'Pronunciation anxiety strikes at all levels of society,' he said. 'When a Cabinet Minister stands up in Parliament and calls someone a "scumsucking dunny rat" it's not that he wants to be unkind, it's just that he's concerned he might mispronounce "irascible reprobate".'

With that moving example, Dr Smythe won my confidence and, in the weeks that followed, helped me take the first tentative steps towards recovery. I'll never forget the moment of our breakthrough. He had me under hypnosis and was explaining that 'riesling' rhymes with 'peas' and not 'pies' and I was explaining that I found this confusing because I preferred a medium-bodied shiraz with peas.

Then, suddenly, out of the blue, I remembered how my pronunciation anxiety had started.

'At the moment of your birth,' asked Dr Smythe excitedly, 'when you heard the obstetrician mispronounce "obstetrician"?'

I shook my head. 'It was on the 27th of July, 1982,' I said, 'when ABC radio pronounced "kilometre" three different ways in the same news item. It caused quite a controversy. Particularly in Monaco.'

Dr Smythe stared at me proudly. 'By Jove,' he said, 'I think he's got it.'

After that there was no holding me back. In a group therapy session I used 'schism', 'scion', 'segue' and 'sciatica' in the same sentence. Nobody had a clue what I was talking about but it didn't matter. Later in the same session I tossed in a casual 'Do you think my dirndl the epitome of chic?', which must have made the others a bit jealous because they voted I be transferred to the psychiatric ward.

Dr Smythe stood by me and soon I was ready to tackle the major American publishers. In one heady, unforgettable week I learned that the Houghton in Houghton Mifflin is pronounced 'Hoeton', that the Schuster in Simon and Schuster is pronounced 'Shooster', and that the Jovanovich in Harcourt Brace Jovanovich was asked to leave the company because people were getting tongue cramps.

Then Dr Smythe announced I was ready to go back to the bookshop. I strode in confidently, Dr Smythe two paces behind with an oxygen mask just in case.

'Hello,' I said to the assistant, 'I'd like a copy of *A Suitable Boy* by Vikram Seth, please.'

The assistant looked at me with shining eyes. 'My hero,' she said. 'You're the first customer to pronounce

Seth, "Sate". Please, would you sign my copy? Put "in memory of a special occasion".'

'OK,' I said, taking her pen. 'Occasion, how do you spell that? Does it have one c and one s, or two c's and two s's?'

My stomach started to churn. The bookshop started to spin.

BLAME

The butler did it.
Agatha Christie

*Blame is bad and we should all stop it immediately.
Trouble is, it's so quick, cheap and convenient. Whereas
taking responsibility for our feelings and acknowledging
that our lives are largely determined by our own
decisions is very hard and really cuts into telly-viewing
time. If you're trying to give up blame, good on you,
and if you should waver and find yourself pointing
the finger at any bureaucrats or committees, I certainly
won't blame you.*

I WANT TO START by apologising. Usually I write for
everyone equally and without favour except for a slight
bias towards those of you who can read.

I'm afraid this chapter is different. This chapter is for

every single one of you equally and without favour as long as you have a connection with the Melbourne municipality of Boroondara.

I hope this won't exclude too many of you. Boroondara covers quite a large area of Melbourne's eastern suburbs, so even if you don't actually live there, I'm hoping you might have some other connection. Relatives perhaps, or a souvenir tea-towel. Maybe its postcode has the same digits as your blood pressure.

If not, I'm sorry. I don't have a connection either. I wish I didn't have to write this chapter. But I just can't leave the poor Boroondarans to their awful fate.

People of Boroondara, something terrible and absurd and crazy is afoot. Your council is thinking of abolishing litter bins. Why? I'll tell you, but first, please, put your heads between your knees and remove all sharp objects from your pockets.

Your council has come across a theory. Abolish litter bins, the theory states, and your litter problem will go away. Now I'm in no position to knock another person's theory, not while my own theory about the origin of stretch marks (swallowed bubblegum) remains unproven. But I've seen the litter theory put into practice. North Sydney Council abolished its litter bins several years ago. It says the move was a big success. I lived in North Sydney for several years, Boroondarans, and I'm writing this to tell you the truth.

I'll never forget the day our bins disappeared. There I was, standing outside a shop with a pine-lime icy pole in one hand and a sticky wrapper in the other. I reached towards my regular bin. It had vanished. My first thought was that aliens had visited Earth to pick up their

ET video royalties from Steven Spielberg, had taken the scenic route home via North Sydney and had curated my litter bin for one of their museums. I could see it in my mind's eye, bathed in a laser spotlight. 'The Human Race's Most Useful Invention', the caption would truthfully record.

Then I realised all the bins in the street were gone. In their place were council signs warning of grave and recently increased penalties for littering. Fines so large that if you paid them in cash you'd be ankle-deep in those strips of brown paper the banks wrap around wads of notes.

Stunned citizens, most with an icy pole in one hand and a sticky wrapper in the other, stared around helplessly. What were we supposed to do with our litter? I noticed a page from a newspaper blowing towards me along the street. As it got closer I read a quote from the mayor. 'Take your litter home.' Jaws hit the ground. We hoped jaws weren't counted as litter.

I wasn't going home that day for about six hours. I had a business meeting, a medical appointment and under-seven footy training. I hadn't planned to make a sticky icy pole wrapper part of any of them. (Except perhaps the business meeting.) And definitely not a soft-drink can or a hot chip box or a flavoured-milk carton or a burger wrapper or the liposuction brochure I picked up in the chemist. I could see my fellow citizens felt the same way.

I'm not going to make any risky admissions here, Boroondarans. Instead I'll just list a few of the places where people in North Sydney, since that day, hide their litter.

1. The exhaust pipes of vehicles (council if possible).
2. Lifts.
3. Airconditioning ducts.
4. Shoes in shoe shops.
5. The mayor's office. (There's a litter bin under the desk.)

So Boroondara Council, please, think again. It'll be easier to do that now than when you're being deafened by backfiring cars and exploding airconditioning units. If you do manage to get people to take their litter home, it won't vanish. Their kids won't eat it. You'll still have to collect it from their place. And meanwhile, come election day, you'll have a new type of litter blowing around your streets. Your how-to-vote cards.

CONTROL

Mind the gap.
London Transport

Control freaks have always had bad press, except those who control newspapers. People don't like other people tidying up the lettuce in their McFeasts when they'd rather have it left straggly. What, tragically, they don't see is that controlling behaviour is often an attempt to express love. A pathetic and morally unjustifiable attempt, sure, but some days it's all we're capable of, particularly if we're parents, pet-owners or authors.

I'VE BEEN SPENDING a lot of time in bookshops lately, browsing. Actually, browsing's not exactly the right word. What's it called when you go into a bookshop and pick up copies of your new book and dust them and give them a little kiss and place them on a more prominent shelf and glare indignantly at customers who aren't buying them? Um . . . that's right, making a nuisance of myself.

Fortunately, bookshop staff are very tolerant. Very few have actually had me arrested. Mostly they just keep a watchful eye on me and leave me alone unless I get out the megaphone.

The thing they hate most is me talking to customers. That's probably what caused the skirmish the other day, me talking to that woman queuing at the till. I was only trying to explain how she wouldn't be missing out on much if she bought my new book instead of *Pride and Prejudice* because my book contains 49 per cent of the actual words to be found in the Jane Austen. And how it'd be around 50 per cent if Jane hadn't been so prudish about using the word dunny.

I must say I was surprised by the woman's response. Okay, I was annoying her a bit, so it was probably natural for her to whack me round the head with a book. But she could have used *Pride and Prejudice* instead of running all the way to the back of the shop to get *War and Peace* in hardback.

The bookshop staff would never have done that because they understand that having a book published is a very stressful experience for authors. Well it is for me, and I'm sure if I ever get the chance to talk to other authors about it, say in a police paddy wagon, they'll agree.

I've never personally had a baby, but I reckon publication must come pretty close. Except for the epidural. (Authors aren't given pain-killers at the actual birth of their book. All medical intervention is delayed for a few weeks until the reviews.)

The booksellers reckon I'm being broodier with this

book than any of my previous ones. Apparently I've always been happy in the past for each of my books to be in a simple paper bag when it leaves the shop with a customer. Apparently this is the first time I've insisted on a warm singlet.

I put this down to my new book's longer than usual gestation period. Each of my previous children's books has taken less than a year to produce, including pencil sharpening. They are, after all, slimmish volumes. I've been whacked round the head with them in bookshops countless times and hardly felt a thing.

This one, on the other hand, took nearly two years. I'd rather not say why here as the details are still a bit painful, but suffice to say that if anyone does find my thesaurus, there's a reward that I can only describe as big, huge, enormous and . . . um . . . big.

The feelings I'm experiencing now can be seen all around us in nature. Naturalists, I think I'm right in saying this, call it Extended Gestation Ochlophobia. (I wish I could be more certain but I left my *Encyclopaedia Britannica* on the same bus as my thesaurus.)

The hampster, for example, which takes only about 16 days to produce its offspring, loses interest in them very soon after birth. Even when the youngsters are suffering food deprivation and are under threat from predators, the parents can still be found curled up somewhere warm with the latest Bryce Courtenay.

The Indian elephant, by contrast, carries its young for a phenomenal 22 months. The care and concern shown by Indian elephants towards their young is legendary. Rarely will you see a young Indian elephant left unattended in a parked car.

Authors are like Indian elephants (except from behind). During the long months and years of our creative confinement we bond with our books for life. Little wonder, then, that come publication we turn into doting parents displaying all the anxious and over-protective symptoms of Extended Gestation Ochlophobia. (Or as it's called in literary circles, EGO.)

So thank you, booksellers, for being so understanding. I've stretched your patience many times, I know, and I understand why sometimes you've had to make me stop talking to your customers. Though I'm still a bit puzzled about why you needed to use quite so much masking tape.

I'd like to offer you a deal. If you let me back into your shops to do a bit of light dusting and install a few spotlights over my shelf, I promise never again to snatch copies of my books from intending purchasers' hands and try to underline the good bits.

I'll go one further. My just-completed book is off to the printers in a few weeks. I promise that when it comes into your stores, I won't be lurking around pestering people. That's because I'll be too exhausted. I've just discovered a whole new area of prenatal responsibility. I was at the printers yesterday and their presses were filthy, absolutely covered in ink. And today I'm off to the paper mill to make sure they've got enough fibre in their wood pulp. A parent's work is never done.

COWARDICE

**No coward soul is mine,
No trembler in the world's
storm-troubled sphere**
Emily Bronte

*If more of us were like Emily Bronte, we
wouldn't have to spend so much on soul-nurturing books
without hymns in them. We try to be brave, we really do.
We face fears and shuffle towards our dreads and tackle
spiders in the kitchen armed only with a tea-towel and
the jaffle-maker. Then, just when we've learned to deal
with the dark places and the slimy stuff, along
comes technology.*

MY CUBMASTER taught me not to be afraid of the
unknown. I've been grateful to him ever since, even
though he did it primarily so I wouldn't ask him what
was in the rissoles at camp.

Thanks to him, I survived a major childhood trauma.

In Year 4, I banged my head on my lunchbox, developed a splitting headache and suddenly the teacher seemed to be writing unintelligible hieroglyphics on the board. I remembered my cubmaster's words and didn't panic. Which was just as well because it was only algebra.

My cubmaster's precious legacy has served me well in adult life, too. Thanks to him, I can reach fearlessly down the back of the fridge for a lost school note, even though I haven't got a clue whether the blue furry thing down there is an old Smurf or an even older rissole.

Thanks to my cubmaster, I've been able to embrace the unknown at every stage of my life. Until a few days ago. Since then it hasn't been quite so easy. I've had to remind myself of his teachings quite frequently. About every three minutes. I'm still doing it now. 'Dib dib dib,' I chant. 'Dob dob dob. I am kin to the fearless wolf and the very brave wombat and none of us is afraid of our new computer.'

I didn't want a new computer. I was perfectly happy with the previous one. It was six years old but it did everything I needed a notebook computer to do. (Almost. It wasn't that good at soaking up lemon cordial.) It was blindingly fast compared to what I was using before. (A blunt pencil.)

Okay, journalists would snigger when I told them I wrote my books on a 286. Kids would look blank and I'd hear their parents explaining to them about quill pens and illuminated manuscripts and 286s. I got begging letters from museums.

But we worked well together, me and the old 286. Until last week, when I was using it on a bus and I heard a pensioner mutter 'old fogey'. I closed it up indignantly and there was an ominous cracking sound. I hoped it was the pensioner eating peanut brittle, but, alas, it wasn't. The plastic casing of my faithful old friend had finally succumbed to age and cordial corrosion.

'Farewell,' I said when I got it home. 'You've earned a long and peaceful retirement.' I put it on the shelf next to my cub cap and the blunt pencil.

'Hooray,' said the kids. 'Dad's going to upgrade his computer at last.'

I shook my head. 'No, I'm not,' I said. 'I'm going to get one exactly the same as the last one except for the Bay City Rollers sticker on the case.'

In the notebook computer shop all the staff seemed to have been replaced since I was last there. A young salesman approached me eagerly. 'It's okay,' I said, 'I know exactly what I want. One 286, and don't bother wrapping it.'

The salesman gave me a very strange look. 'Sorry, sir', he said, 'they don't make 286s any more.' He grinned and gave me a nudge. 'Oh, and before you ask, we don't sell quill pens either.'

I sighed. It looked like I was going to be forced to keep up with the times. 'Okay,' I said, resigned, 'I'll take a 287.'

The salesman gave me an even stranger look. 'No such thing,' he said.

I was stunned. Why on earth not? All I could think was that fundamentalist groups had prevented it from being manufactured after discovering the numerals 287 had satanic significance. Perhaps it was Stephen King's street number.

'Okay,' I said, 'I'll take a 288, as long as it doesn't

have any more memory than my old one. It makes me nervous when a computer has a better memory than me.'

The salesman swapped glances with his colleagues, who were obviously impressed by my ability to take huge technological changes in my stride. I told them my last computer had a 20-megabyte hard disk and one megabyte of RAM. 'I'd like the same on the 288, please,' I said firmly.

For some reason, the salesman and his colleagues all developed breathing problems at the same time. Heavy smokers, probably. 'Actually, sir,' said the salesman when he'd recovered the power of speech, 'our slowest notebook is a Pentium 266.'

'That's ridiculous,' I said. 'I don't want to downgrade. Well, not that much. I might settle for a 270. But only if the operating speed can keep up with my old one. That was 12 megaherz, you know.'

'Sir,' said the salesman after another long bout of choking, 'would you like to sit down?'

I sat down. He then told me that the Pentium 266 operated at 266 megaherz with 32 megabytes of RAM and a range of hard disk sizes starting at 840 megabytes and going up to 3,600 megabytes. I fainted.

I'm writing this with the blunt pencil. My new computer's sitting up the other end of the desk. After singing lots of cub songs, I got brave enough to switch it on. The screen exploded into colour, music played and dozens of little pictures appeared. The computer has obviously decided that pictures are all I'm capable of comprehending. Just as well, I guess. With that much memory, it probably knows some really long words.

One of the pictures is of a small insect. I think that's Pentium pictorial language for New Owner. I haven't been game to switch off my new computer because I think it's watching me.

My new computer can store 200 million names and addresses. That's good. In there somewhere will be my old cubmaster's address. Now I can drop him a note.

'Help.'

CYNICISM

Cynicism is intellectual dandyism.
George Meredith

*I prefer a kinder, less cynical view. Could cynicism not
simply be an attempt by nervous and vulnerable folk
to hide behind a protective veneer of world-weariness?
Or its post-modern substitute, irony?*

SORRY IF I SEEM a bit tense, but six days, three hours and
27 minutes ago I gave up the habit that's provided me
with pleasure and consolation for most of my adult life.
You know the habit I mean. Bad for the health. Kids do
it to look tough. People reckon it puts them off their food
when other people do it near them in restaurants. That's
right, I've given up cynicism.

It's not an easy thing to give up after more than 30 years.
Closer to 31 if you count the two weeks I spent in hospital
after treading on that garden rake lent to me by that very

generous bloke next door who just happened by pure co-incidence to drive a truck for a surgical supply company and whose wife almost certainly wasn't studying to be a speech therapist specialising in remedial programs for people with lengths of wood up their noses.

Phew, that was close. We ex-cynics have to be on our guard the whole time. Yesterday, for example. One minute I was on the phone listening to a Telstra ad while I waited for a service consultant to answer my call, the next minute the terrible craving started and I found myself on the brink of taking up cynicism again.

Appallingly cynical thoughts danced alluringly on my mental horizon. Obviously I can't write them here because I didn't allow myself to think them, but suffice to say they involved (a) a certain telecommunications corporation knowing that keeping its customers waiting on the line for 15 or 20 minutes at a time gives it a whizzo marketing opportunity, and (b) rooms full of service consultants sitting around with their feet up making origami phone boxes while they wait for the customers on the line to hear the requisite 47 ads each.

Fortunately I was able to jump under a cold shower before the thoughts took hold, but I shudder at what my fate would have been otherwise. Particularly as the next ad after I'd turned the tap on was the third repeat of a reminder to make some off-peak international calls very soon as 'there are only 168 hours in a week'.

If I hadn't been preoccupied with the soap bubbles coming out of my phone, I'd almost certainly have succumbed to the deep satisfaction of a cynical mutter. Probably something about how there are actually 216 hours in a week, at least for people who don't need to contact Telstra service consultants. Something like that. Though I can't be sure because instead of muttering I stuck soap in my ears and yodelled.

I have to admit that some days life can seem a bit empty without a cynical mutter, particularly for someone like me who was on 40 a day. But I had a powerful reason to quit. The kids. I was worried they were picking up the habit from me. More and more I'd noticed their response to a confusing and uncertain modern world was a cynical one.

'Come on,' I'd say, 'let's go outside and play with the birds and the insects and the flowers.'

Their eyes would narrow. 'Dad,' they'd mutter, 'it's midnight and it's raining.'

It pained me to see youthful optimism and exuberance so constrained. Specially when they locked me in the laundry.

I was also concerned about the effect such narrow pessimism would have on their future careers. As companies shun the hard-heartedness of the old century and encourage sensitivity and humanity in their employees, cynics have become the new pariahs. You see them, huddled in groups outside office buildings, often smoking to keep warm, muttering things like 'don't let that blue sky fool you, the carbon monoxide level's 87,' and 'who's that bugger writing down everything we say, the one with the rake handle up his nose?'

I'm delighted to see that my self-denial is paying off and the kids are starting to follow my example. This morning, for example, I showed them the jar of cellulite control complex I'd just bought.

'Look,' I said excitedly, 'a fast-acting, ultra-penetrating

gel that produces silky smooth skin texture in a matter of weeks.'

Their new-found trust and open-mindedness were deeply touching. 'It sounds great,' they said. They did frown a little bit, but only when they asked me if I was sure I should be eating it.

And it's not just the kids that have benefited. My days seem rosier too, now that I spend them thinking the best of people. It's a lovely feeling, knowing I can relax playing Monopoly with Alan Bond and place Bill Clinton's autobiography with confidence on the non-fiction shelf. Having to give up my seat on a Spanish bus to the tragically ill Christopher Skase is a small price to pay for such serenity.

But I mustn't get complacent. The craving can return at any time. The other day I went to the airport to meet someone on a domestic flight operated by One Of The World's Great Airlines. Being free of all cynicism I got there at the advertised arrival time. An hour-and-a-half later the flight landed. Soon after, in the airport carpark queue, the man in the next car saw me groping desperately under my seat for $14.

'That's why the flights are always late,' he said. 'The profit margins on discount air fares are so low they need the extra carpark fees.'

I wound up my window as fast as I could. I'd heard about the dangers of passive cynicism.

We sat in the queue for another five minutes. By the time I got to the cashier's booth the charge was $17. 'That's why there are so few booths,' said the man in the next car. After a long and painful struggle I resisted the temptation to agree with him. When, oh when, are they going to finally ban cynicism in public places?

DECEiT

**Every Australian will have equal
access to tickets.**

*Olympic ad
(paraphrased)*

OK, I admit it, I tell lies too. None of them has ever
involved the allocation of tickets to a major sporting
event but I have knowingly deceived people.
As we all, wincingly and tied in internal
knots, have. How, for example, would you
answer the following questions?

1

'Daddy, will you stay married to Mummy for ever and
ever and ever, promise, promise, promise?'

2

'Just as a matter of interest, have you ever
enjoyed sex more with anyone else?'

3

'It's me, your oldest friend, the one who's
a member of the SOCOG Committee. I need
to know, do you still respect me?'

*Don't be too hard on yourself. One day we'll
evolve into a completely honest species. Only problem
will be, we won't have ears.*

MY OFFICE RANG with the sounds of industry. The fax
hummed, the hard disk whirred, the printer complained
loudly about the cost of its ink cartridges, the stapler
stapled, the sticky tape dispenser dispensed and the tip
of my pencil scratched busily across that itchy bit of skin
behind my left ear.

To anyone passing I must have sounded like the
busiest writer since Stephen King signed a $9 million six-
book contract the same year he put vinyl tiles down on
his patio.

To anyone, that is, except the kids.

'Oh dear,' they said, coming in with worried expres-
sions. 'All this noise can only mean one thing.'

I leaned back at my desk and put down my pencil
and stapler and tape dispenser and three retractable ball-
points, the loud ones, and the automatic pencil sharpener
I got in Jakarta that's powered by a two-stroke motor.

'It means,' I said, 'that I'm very, very busy.'

The kids shook their heads sadly. 'It means,' said the
13-year-old, 'that your brain's seized up and you haven't
got a clue what to write about and we're all going to starve.'

I stared at them, horrified. How had they guessed? I'd
been making all the hard-working noise of a person who
was close to finishing his second novel since breakfast.

'It was the little things that gave you away,' said the
10-year-old. 'You forgot to plug the hard disk into
the computer, and the printer's just produced its thirty-
eighth page covered with your Medicare number, and

judging by the crumbs in the fax machine you've been copying toast again.'

'Plus,' said his sister, 'the itchy bit of skin's behind your right ear, not your left.'

'But most of all,' said her brother, 'we knew what you were doing because we do it ourselves at school. Everyone does it. When the teacher walks past your desk you puff and sigh a lot to make it sound as though you're thinking.'

I nodded, remembering. 'And grind your teeth,' I said, 'and hold your breath till you turn blue and hit yourself on the head with a wooden pencil case.'

The kids gave me a strange look but I barely noticed because I'd had an awful thought. What if I wasn't the only one who'd carried the practice into adulthood? What if half the noise in the world is made by people trying to sound busier than they really are? No wonder earplug production is one of the few bright spots in the economy.

The kids went into the next room and switched on the TV (they obviously wanted me to think they were busy doing their homework) and I went out to test this awful hypothesis. Before I reached the end of the street I heard a familiar roar. A gardener wearing industrial earmuffs was blowing leaves around the forecourt of a block of units with a power blower.

The noise was painful. I'd heard low-flying 747s shift leaves more quietly. And the work was futile. As the gardener laconically blew the leaves one way, a strong westerly (probably the result of a concentration of power blowers to the west) blew them back again. But the residents of the block were probably thinking what a hard-working gardener they'd hired, even though they had to think it cowering in their wardrobes with socks stuffed in their ears.

Round the corner was a traffic jam. Huge trucks sat motionless, engines revving impatiently. In the past as I've sat behind them, their vibrations shaking the St Rufus medal off my dashboard (he's the patron saint of rust), I've imagined productivity-obsessed truck drivers anxious to get their load of earplugs to Brisbane. Now another possibility occurred to me. That in those high cabs the knights of the road were having a quick kip while trained kelpies jumped up and down on the accelerator pedals.

Next morning, after a hard night at the keyboard trying to think of something to write about, I was woken as usual at seven by the scream of power tools from the building site near my place. In the past I've shrugged my sleep-deprived shoulders and stumbled towards the aspirin, consoled by the thought that at least a better Australia was being built for our kids. (Always assuming our kids have $850,000 to buy a classic Federation with Cape Cod extension.)

That morning I was gripped by darker thoughts. Could it be that building supervisors tend to make their pre-ten a.m. site inspections by phone? Could it be therefore that my sleep was being shattered by circular saws and servo-assisted bevels left running as an aural smoke-screen throughout a leisurely on-site brekkie?

I rang the council to complain. All I could hear down the phone were those sounds we've come to recognise as synonymous with an office working flat out. The electronic three-note version of *Greensleeves*.

As the second movement started and I waited in vain for a human voice, or even a human musician, the full horror of what I had stumled on hit home. The biggest industry in the world isn't plastics or food processing or Pokémon, it's the manufacture of sound effects. Computer printers, electric toothbrushes, motel beds, passenger planes, lawn-mowers and toasted muesli all make the racket they do only because we want people to hear us using them.

This truth was too big for one man to live with. I had to share it with the world. I flung open the window and shouted it at the top of my lungs across the rooftops. For a long moment the suburb held its breath, digesting my message. Then, from a nearby block of units, came a lone voice asking me to keep the noise down.

DELUSIONS

I'm the king of the world.
James Cameron, Director, Titanic
Oscar acceptance speech

Most of us are brought up to believe the world is full of icebergs and we're on our own personal Titanic. ('Be careful', 'Watch out', 'You'll be sorry', 'Now look what you've done. You've broken a 90,000-tonne ocean liner and killed 1500 people.') The icy waters of life can be a scary place to sail. Little wonder we develop a heroic delusion or two.

WHEN I WAS NINE, I started turning into John Wayne. At first it wasn't that obvious – just a hint of a swagger and a US marshal badge pinned to my chest during every waking moment. Which made bathtime pretty painful.

But the more John Wayne movies I saw, the more he

took over my life. I started insisting people call me The Duke. Or Marion. I spent hours mastering the lasso. By the time I was 10, I could corral any guinea pig that'd stay still for more than two minutes – three if the rope still had washing on it. I started chewing tobacco, and when I couldn't get tobacco, I'd lick ashtrays.

I'll never forget swaggering out of *How the West Was Won* with Wayne's distinctive rolling gait and wondering if he walked like that because he too had a plastic holster that stuck to his leg and made his shorts ride up. I asked the usherette about this in his distinctive drawl. She didn't understand, probably because my front three teeth were missing so it was more of a drool. I didn't care. I went to the nearest rocky outcrop and threw myself with a fearless cry on to a passing Comanchero. Luckily for me, bikies were quite tolerant in those days.

The most exciting hours of my adolescence were the ones I spent watching *The War Wagon*, *Hellfighters*, *True Grit* and *A Midsummer Night's Dream*. (That last one was a mistake. When I read in the review about the Duke wearing tights, I rushed straight out and bought a ticket.)

I'm not sure now what finally broke the spell. News that Wayne had started to wear a girdle, perhaps, and Mum's refusal to lend me one. Or perhaps it was the lousy service I got in my local Vietnamese restaurant once I took to wearing that green beret.

Whatever it was, one day I realised I was no longer John Wayne. I couldn't be, because I was Dustin Hoffman. I'd just seen *The Graduate* and, in two hours, my life had changed. Here at last was a hero without a hair on his chest. Even more exciting, the close-ups showed that, like me, he didn't even have follicles in that area.

I was captivated. A hero I could emulate, even in rooms with mirrors. Plus, I mused as I left the cinema with Dustin's distinctive anaemic slouch, a hero who shared my bad posture and love of high-pitched singing. (The moment I first heard Simon and Garfunkel I knew they'd had plastic holsters.)

I emulated Dustin in every way I could. I spent days in deep introspection. It wasn't hard because I already knew the required facial expression. It was the one John Wayne used when he looked down and saw he had an arrow in his leg.

I saw *The Graduate* another 16 times and took to holding my breath in the local swimming pool for long periods of time. People thought I was crazy. It had been drained for the winter.

I didn't care. For the first time in my life, I had an ambition: to meet a woman called Mrs Robinson. Following Dustin's example, I set out to meet her daughter first. On university enrolment day, I hung hopefully around the desk marked R-S. Only after nine hours did I realise the sign meant the desk was broken.

Then the American singer Smokey Robinson came to town. In a fever of excitement, but careful not to let it spoil my pallid languor, I bought a ticket. After the concert I snuck into his dressing room. His mother was there. She was 94. She told me I should get some colour into my cheeks and suggested I try chewing tobacco.

Then, as abruptly as the whole thing had started, one day I suddenly knew I was no longer Dustin Hoffman. I'd just seen *Marathon Man* and I was at the dentist for a checkup. The dentist told me he'd have to drill. In the seconds that followed, I told him where the diamonds were (South Africa mostly, with a few mines in Brazil) and which of my relatives were in the CIA. (Aunty Gwen. Not true, but I was desperate.) It was a shameful performance, but it saved me a fortune in cosmetics when *Tootsie* was released.

The years passed and I waited for another screen hero to occupy my psyche. It didn't happen. I did drive a car that displayed the number 007 for a few months, but only because the trip meter was broken. I did say 'I'll be back' a few times at one stage, but only because I was negotiating which part of the school fete donkey I'd be.

Screen heroes have come and gone, and I've remained strangely unaffected. Until recently. I didn't even notice what was happening at first. I thought the hair loss was just the result of genetics and wearing a cowboy hat too young. I thought my swelling midriff was just the result of too many calories. (Nobody told me that when you chew tobacco you're not meant to swallow it.)

Okay, I have been watching a lot of TV lately, but only because they've been showing so many John Wayne and Dustin Hoffman movies. And I have developed a big appetite for bacon, cheese slices, doughnuts and ribs, but not always in the same meal.

So you can imagine how surprised I was at dinner the other night when, just after I mistakenly ate a cheese slice with the wrapper on and said 'Doh', the kids gave a loud wail.

'Oh no,' they cried, 'Dad's turning into Homer Simpson.'

I was indignant. Bitterly so. In my mind I formulated a carefully structured argument listing my many intellectual, artistic, humanist and cultural qualities. As dessert arrived I opened my mouth and let them have it.

'Mmmmm,' I said, 'chocolate chip.'

DENiAL

No fear.
Clothing brand

*We're allowed to protect our bodies with airbags,
insurance policies, handrails, emergency exits, 30+
blockout and double-strength condoms. Why shouldn't
we be allowed to protect our psyches with a little
bit of denial?*

IT CAME TO ME at the traffic lights, a blinding moment
of realisation. 'Yes!' I shouted, pounding the steering
wheel with my fists.

'Please don't do that,' said the driver.

I grabbed him by the shoulders. 'You don't understand,' I cried, 'I've just discovered why my life is so
problem-filled and anxiety-ridden. It's because I'm in the
wrong profession.'

The driver sighed. 'We're all in the wrong profession,' he said, 'so be quiet and move down the bus.'

The university administration officer was more sympathetic.

'Hello,' I said. 'I'd like a job, please.'

She checked her computer. 'Nothing at the moment,' she said with a friendly smile, 'but we do have vacancies from time to time. What did you have in mind? Cleaner? Storeman? Carpark attendant?'

'Revisionist historian,' I said. 'I have a burning desire to re-examine past events in the light of redefined ideologies, revised modes of discourse and updated theories of memory and recall.'

The administration officer looked at me doubtfully. 'The academic requirements are pretty stringent,' she said. 'What history qualifications do you have?'

I stared at the floor. 'Well,' I mumbled, 'the traditional view is that I failed Unit One Convicts And Squatters at Bathurst Teachers' College, but there is a revisionist position which says I actually hold doctorates from Harvard, Cambridge and Leningrad, plus a fan-club membership certificate from *Countdown*.'

'And who supports this position?' asked the officer.

I took a deep breath. 'I do,' I said.

'Good,' she smiled. 'You're obviously qualified for the job. Fill out this form and we'll let you know if anything comes up.'

Flushed with success, I hurried home to start my new life as a revisionist historian. The plumber was just finishing in the kitchen. He handed me his bill. It read 'Removal of foreign object from sink waste-disposal unit, 27.3 hrs @ $65 per hr, $1,774.50.'

'This means you've been here since 10 o'clock yester-day morning,' I said nervously.

'Give or take,' he said.

'But,' I pleaded, 'I only called you at midday today.'

The plumber scowled. I recognised it as the expression of a man who was about to insert a foreign object back into a sink waste-disposal unit. I wavered. Every fibre in my body wanted to write out the cheque, thank him profusely and carry his plunger out to his ute. But somehow I managed to get the words out. 'I think,' I said, 'you should re-contextualise your data parameters.'

The blood drained from his face. 'Aw jeez,' he stammered, 'you're a revisionist historian.'

I nodded. 'Eighty bucks,' he whimpered, 'and I'll wipe the dirty finger marks off the sink.'

After he'd gone I went to the service centre to pick up my car. 'Good news, Mr Gleitzman,' beamed the counter assistant. 'We found the problem and she's all fixed.'

I studied the account. 'Investigate and rectify poor acceleration,' it said. 'Replace engine and gearbox. Parts $3,946. Labour $2,430.'

This is outrageous.' I said.

'How do you know?' demanded the service manager, coming out of his office. 'When you brought the car in you said you didn't know what the problem was.'

'Well,' I said. 'I've taken the recorded modules of occurrence of that day and applied a post-structuralist paradigm and I am now prepared to support the view that the engine was coughing because I dropped one of the spark plugs down the sink when I was rinsing it under the tap.'

There was a long silence. Then the service manager

turned to the assistant. 'I've told you before,' he hissed, 'not to try it on with revisionist historians.'

I drove away revelling in my new-found power. And I'm ashamed to say, as has happened so often in human history, it went to my head. (Though I am prepared to countenance the view that it actually went to my lymph glands.)

I rang my mother and told her it wasn't me who wet the bed on September 22, 1962, it was a lawn sprinkler dropped from a Martian spaceship. 'That's amazing,' she said, 'I've just been reading in the paper about a history professor from Bonn University who had the same thing happen to him last week.'

I wrote a monograph challenging conclusively the long-held notion that between 1970 and 1983 Doug Hinkley and I played 14,633 games of table tennis and Doug won them all. After he'd read the monograph, Doug was stunned. 'A semiotic paradigm-shift,' he said, shaking his head, 'and I always thought it was because you had lousy back-spin.'

Then I went to see Mr Wilson, my high-school history teacher, to explain the principles of revisionism to him and accept his apology for giving my final-year essay a D-minus just because it claimed that Henry VIII was a movie starring Sylvester Stallone.

Mr Wilson was delighted to see me. 'Come in, dear boy,' he said, ushering me inside.

'I'm not disturbing you, am I?' I asked.

'Heavens no,' he chuckled, 'I was just tinkering with my latest book. It's a slim volume which proves conclusively that World War II never happened, that it was merely a fiction perpetrated by some Jews who wanted to make war

46

movies. And what about you Gleitzman, what profession have you chosen?'

'Me?' I stammered as I backed away, groping desperately for the door handle. 'I'm having a mid-life career change. I've just decided to be a bus driver.'

DiShOnESTY

**We regret any inconvenience caused by
our late departure.**
Daily airline announcement

*Ethicists hold truth to be the holy grail. Philosophers are
pretty keen on it too, even though they don't know
exactly what it is. The rest of us, circling in the complex
holding patterns of our lives, are sometimes tempted to
sacrifice truth for nobler outcomes.*

IN THE WEEKS leading up to the 1996 Sex Pistols tour
there was more pleading and begging at our place than
in the average toy shop. 'Please, they may never come to
Australia again, at least not without geriatric nursing
staff who'll deaden the sound.' Finally the tears and the
sleeve-tugging worked. The kids said I could go.

'On one condition,' they added on the night of the
concert. 'That you don't embarrass us.'

I was so indignant my hair would have bristled if it hadn't already been set into spikes with Polyfilla and food colouring. 'I'll have you know,' I said, 'I was there. I was present at the birth of punk.'

The kids were impressed. 'You were at the Pistols' first gig in London in the '70s?' they asked.

I unhooked the chain from my nose so I could answer without rattling. 'Not their very first gig,' I replied, 'but I was there the night they played Amsterdam.'

The kids' eyes widened. 'Unreal,' they breathed.

'It was,' I agreed. 'I was on a Windmill & Tulip package tour and the noise from the stadium was so loud it made the little china salt and pepper clogs rattle on my table at the Oostelijk Holiday Inn.'

The kids were suddenly less impressed, but I didn't care. Here at last was a chance to bond with them musically through the one group we both had a link to. The Sex Pistols could help us get closer in a way we'd never achieved during all the years of the kids trying to get me to like Nirvana and me trying to get them to like The Ronettes.

As long as I didn't embarrass them. 'Don't be a Nigel, Dad,' they said. I knew what a Nigel was. There'd been one at the Nimbin Rock Festival when I was 19. 'Excuse me,' he'd said to the stoned roadie meditating in the pool of mud backstage, 'I don't seem to be able to find an usherette to show me to my seat.' I shudder to think of it even now. Particularly the way the roadie looked at me.

The key to not embarrassing anybody, I said to myself as we queued outside the Sex Pistols concert, is authenticity. That and not getting your ripped jeans tangled up in the turnstile.

Fortunately one of the security guards had a spanner, so I was soon free and heading for the refreshments counter. I glanced around to make sure the kids were in earshot. 'Giss a beer, snotrag,' I said to the bloke serving. I actually don't like beer that much, but I wanted something to spit at the boys on stage. I know toothpaste's cheaper, but it doesn't have the same cred.

The bloke behind the bar finished serving some other people and turned to me. 'I said giss a beer, phlegm-face,' I snarled. I glanced over at the kids. They were at the next counter buying souvenir T-shirts without using any unpleasant or abrasive language at all. Poor loves, I thought, they're shy.

'Where's my beer, scum-head?' I hissed at the bloke behind the bar.

'Sorry, sir,' he said, 'we can't serve you unless you're wearing a plastic wristband to show that your ID has been verified and you are indeed over 18.'

I stared at him in disbelief. 'I'm 43, scab-brain,' I said. 'I'm a parent and ratepayer.'

He shrugged. 'Sorry, sir,' he said, 'those are the rules.'

I made one of the rips in my jeans bigger. 'Look,' I said, 'varicose veins.'

He shook his head.

My nose chain was rattling with exasperation. 'I was at the Nimbin Rock Festival,' I said.

He didn't seem to hear me. 'The ID verification office is over there,' he said, pointing.

'Fascist,' I muttered.

In the queue outside the office I noticed that the young couple behind me were staring at my authentic punk outfit. They were dressed in drab black T-shirts and jeans, and were obviously upset that their own shredded singlets and mutilated straitjackets hadn't come back from the cleaners in time.

I called the kids over and tried to get a chant going in the queue to register our anarchic rage. 'No future, no future, no future for tardy members of the garment-care industries,' I chanted.

Everyone ignored me, including the couple behind. 'Wassa matter?' I asked. 'Your squat so damp you've lost your voices?'

The young woman handed me an embossed card. 'Actually,' she said, 'I'm an immunologist and that safety pin looks as though it's infecting your ear.'

Before I could make an appointment to see her, a voice called 'next' and I realised I was at the head of the queue. I handed my driver's licence to the security officer in the booth. He looked at the licence photo, at me, at the photo again and at me again. 'Sorry, sir.' he said, 'this licence is obviously stolen and we'll have to hand you over to the police.'

An hour later the police finally let me go, but only after I'd let them suck my hair to prove it was food colouring and I'd successfully named all seven numbers performed by Max Merritt And The Meteors at the Nimbin Rock Festival.

Everyone had gone into the concert, including the kids. The only person left was a bloke of about my age looking as ridiculous as me with his hair spiked green and yellow. He was having a quick smoke and looked as dejected as I felt.

'We're too old for this caper, eh?' I said.

'Bleedin' right,' he said.

51

We stood side by side, arms folded over our paunches, reflecting.

'Oh well,' he said, 'can't stand around here nattering all bleeding night, I'm due on stage.'

I decided not to stay for the concert. There was a tulip documentary on telly.

DISLOYALTY

Australia, your chicken is ready.
TV ad

We used to be told we owed loyalty to God, Queen and Country. We went along with that, knowing our true loyalty belonged to friends, footy team and our favourite fruit shop. Then the marketing industry, buying cumquats one day, discovered loyalty. And now these days I find myself making mainly Disloyalty Pledges.

I HAVEN'T GOT a Fly Buys card. Or a Telstra Optus Qantas Ansett card. I know I'm silly. I know the skies could be opening up for me each time I buy a can of baked beans or a bottle of airsickness tablets.

But I just can't do it. I haven't got any of the loyalty cards. Not even the card my local video store hands out which states that every time you rent three

Tarantinoesque comedy–thrillers with ironic violence you get a fourth one free.

It's not that I've got a problem with loyalty as such. As a kid I was very loyal. If I got some lollies I always shared them with my friends, even the ones who had moved 200 kilometres away.

My loyalty was much remarked on by teachers, which is why in school plays I was always cast as a dog. My performance as Lady Macbeth's Spot still brings tears to the eyes of those who were there, even though I personally found it very gruelling.

In my retail habits I'm extremely loyal. If I find a brand of pool chlorine I like, I stick with it year in and year out, which I think is really loyal because I haven't got a swimming pool.

Disloyalty is not something I've ever been accused of. As the man in the pool shop remarked only last week, 'Disloyal? You? No way. Dopey, yes, but not disloyal.'

And cardwise, I'm not disloyal either, just a bit distrustful. It's myself I don't trust. I know what I'd be like prowling the supermarket clutching a loyalty card. I'd be making purchase decisions purely on the basis of travel goals. How many litres of milk do I need to get to Great Keppel? This tube of tomato paste, forget the nutritional content, how many air centimetres is it worth? Which will get me to Noumea faster: the muesli or the cornflakes with the free plastic hijacker's mask in the box?

I don't know the exact details, but it does seem to take an awful lot of loyalty to get airborne. I see people at the checkout each week pushing trolleys loaded with bottles of suntan lotion, but they're always there the next week and they still haven't got a suntan.

The social implications of all this worry me a bit. If there are millions of loyal shoppers out there, all moving with grim determination, fish finger by fish finger, towards a free flight, what will happen when they all get one? Huge numbers of people spend roughly the same on groceries each week, so a few years down the track there could be a sudden massive demand for tickets. Matched by a sudden massive drop in the demand for fish fingers.

Will the airports be permanently full of disgruntled loyalists clutching their Fly Buys tickets and watching all the full planes fly by?

I suppose not if the airlines buy lots of new planes. Big ones with wide seats, because most of their passengers will be people who've spent the past few years forcing down an extra packet of lamingtons each mealtime for the points.

But what if Ansett buys six new 747s on its Telstra Qantas Visa card? Qantas will have to buy six new 757s just to give Ansett its free flights. It could all get tragically out of hand.

And even if it doesn't, what about those low-income shoppers, no less loyal than the better-off ones, who simply aren't ever going to earn enough air miles for even the shortest scheduled flight? Who won't even get to Canberra or Ballarat or Dubbo? New cities will have to be built on the outskirts of Sydney and Melbourne just to give their extremely short flights somewhere to land.

And what about the very poor? The ones whose few pathetic points, scrimped for and hoarded, aren't even enough to get them to the end of the runway? I don't even want to think about it.

Instead, I'm writing to the big companies suggesting a new type of consumer loyalty program. It's the one politicians use. Remember what they say when they've just been voted in?

'Thanks to all our supporters but now we're going to govern for all Australians.'

Why can't Coles, Ansett, Telstra, Optus, Qantas et al do the same?

'Thanks to all our customers but now we're going to give free flights to all Australians.'

The swimming pool on Great Keppel will get very crowded, but I'd be happy to take up some extra chlorine.

EMBARRASSMENT

**No more unsightly bulges or
embarrassing flab.**
Ad for exercise machine

*Flushing of the face and neck, stimulation of the sweat
glands, increased heart rate and blood circulation,
involuntary movement of the legs – if embarrassment's
meant to be so bad, how come it's so similar to orgasm?*

I MOVED HOUSE recently. I had hoped to give you a detailed account of the whole operation. The neatly packed cartons each containing items from the same domestic group or sub-group. The intricate floor plan showing the correct position in the new house for everything including fluff. The deeply satisfying moment at the end of the day when the removalists joined us for a beer and said it was the best-organised move they'd ever done and insisted on paying us.

Unfortunately, I can't give you any of those details. I can't even tell you with absolute certainty whether the removalists used a truck or a large supermarket trolley. It's all been a bit of a blur since I skidded on a pile of Lego in the new bathroom and tripped over the hedge trimmer under the sink and banged my head on the microwave in the shower cubicle.

All I can recall now are a few confused images, mostly of the bottoms falling out of badly packed cartons, and a few half-remembered emotions. These are all I've got to cling to in my desperate attempt to piece together a lost weekend and find out where I put the toaster.

I'm pretty sure I experienced feelings of confidence at some stage. The kids have just shown me a snap they took of me kneeling in the old driveway next to some of our white goods. The gesture I was making certainly looks confident. Either that or I'd just crushed both thumbs under the washing machine.

Trepidation. I know I felt it, but when and why? Was it when the cardboard boxes arrived and I realised the lounge suite wasn't going to fit into any of them? Or was it when the removalists arrived and immediately asked for coffee? I had no trouble remembering where I'd packed the kettle (in the sock drawer) and the coffee (in the socks), but I couldn't for the life of me remember where I'd packed the mugs. (In the washing machine, as I later discovered. When I tried to wash the socks.)

As I say, these emotions are only half-remembered, but I'm pretty sure anxiety was one of them. Even now, when I think of my possessions being seized by rough uncaring hands, my stomach gives a jolt. (Though that could be the huge quantities of caffeine I'm absorbing through my feet.)

A blurred memory is coming into focus. Me hyperventilating as my white shirts got mixed up with my black ones. It was my fault. I should never have let the kids carry that wardrobe down the stairs.

I remember embarrassment, too. Everybody feels embarrassed at some stage during a move, even rich people who can afford boxes with flaps. There's something about having your settee plonked upside down in the street. Specially when you see the chocolate doughnut squashed onto the bottom. The neighbour's kids thought it was hilarious when I tried to stuff it all into my mouth. (Okay, not quite all. I couldn't fit a couple of the cushions in or the wooden frame.)

The removalists worked hard to save me from further embarrassment. Only once did I see them exchange a subtle glance, dig each other in the ribs, slap their thighs and go purple in the face. This was when they noticed the piano straps across my chest. I'm still not sure what amused them so much. The contrast between the thick straps and my puny sternum, perhaps, or the fact that we haven't got a piano.

Not all the emotions of that tumultuous day were painful ones. I can clearly remember walking through the empty rooms once I'd wrestled the last piece of furniture out of the house. (Piano straps are wonderful for shifting lampshades.) Relief flooded through me as I saw the removalists hadn't missed a single item. Except one. A brown shag-pile bath mat left inexplicably in the kitchen. Angrily, I confronted the head removalist. Patiently, he explained that it wasn't a bath mat, it was the fungal growth from under the fridge.

'Nonsense,' I said, 'it's a bath mat,' and I sprinkled

water on it to demonstrate its absorbent qualities. Then I noticed it wasn't absorbing, it was drinking.

The nausea, I dimly remember, lasted all the way to the new house, which was just as well because when we got there the removalists sadly informed us that my desk wouldn't fit through the door. Feverishly I checked to see if any chocolate doughnuts were increasing its width.

They weren't. I reviewed my options.

1. Set up office in the front yard.
2. Dismantle the desk.
3. Cancel the move and go back to the old house.

I decided on Option 3. Wiser souls suggested I try Option 2. I called for a chainsaw. Wiser souls suggested I try a screwdriver. I borrowed one from our new neighbour and told him I'd only need it for a few minutes. Wiser souls suggested it might be a few days as the dining table, bed, video cabinet, fridge and washing machine wouldn't fit through the door either.

That's when the emotion I remember best set in. Despair is hard to forget, specially when your tears shrink your piano straps and you have difficulty breathing.

But out of despair, I've learned, can grow determination. I've almost got the video cabinet dismantled, with only the fridge and washing machine to go. I'm learning patience, too. When passers-by stop and stare and ask, 'Are you moving?' I don't chuck bits of desk at them any more. I just remember the trepidation and the anxiety and the embarrassment and the tears, and say quietly, 'No, I've been moved enough for one week.'

FAILURE

**He has not learnt his work well and is slow,
if not sleepy, at answering in class.**
Year 7 school report (mine)

*Failure, a wise old biology teacher once explained to me,
is nature's way of reminding us that we haven't done our
homework. It is also, he continued, nature's way of
reminding us of our mortality. That our attempts to live
forever aren't going to be successful, no matter how
much homework we do. Thirty years later I still
remember that conversation with gratitude, mostly
because I still haven't finished my maths assignment.*

WE'VE GOT a new addition to the family and it hasn't
been easy. It never is, of course. Even though our last
new arrival was quite a few years ago, I can still remember the long nights lying awake, ears straining, praying
those soft gurgles wouldn't turn into something more

raucous and ear-shattering. It seems crazy now, all that anxiety over a new fridge.

I've been even more tense this time, as one tends to when the new member of the family is made of flesh and blood. And other bodily fluids. It started the first day we brought our little bundle of joy home. We put her down carefully on the carpet so she could get used to her surroundings and admire the bevelled skirting, and within seconds the carpet was sodden.

'Those nappy manufacturers ought to be shot,' I muttered angrily. 'They promise the world with their elasticised gussets and the first time we put one on our little mite, she's got Niagara Falls running down her leg. How can they justify it, that's what I'd like to know.'

The kids looked at me levelly. 'Easily,' they said. 'You've used a nappy designed for an eight-kilo baby and she's a two-and-a-half kilo dog.'

Weeks passed and things deteriorated. Particularly the carpet. And my attempts at house-training. 'Do it in the proper place,' I'd say gently but firmly, 'or you can't watch *Home & Away*.' The dog would look up at me with her moist, intelligent eyes and pee on my foot. I couldn't understand it. That method had worked first time with the kids.

I became desperate. 'Please,' I pleaded with her. 'We can't go on like this. There are moves to have the living-room carpet declared a protected wetland. You must give us a signal when you need to go. Growl, whine, cross your legs and wince, chew one of my best shoes to a pulp, anything.'

She looked at me for several minutes. Then she chewed one of my best shoes to a pulp. 'Good girl,' I said and whisked her outside.

As we walked around the block, I warned passers-by. 'Keep back,' I shouted. 'Beneath that cute little fluffy exterior, there's a bladder the size of Port Kembla.' I needn't have worried. During the entire block, I wasn't peed on once. Neither was the footpath. We went around another 17 times. Nothing. Exhausted, we staggered indoors. Within seconds, the kitchen floor was awash.

I watched the thin, acid-smelling lake lap against Dougie (the fridge) and then I snapped. I grabbed the dog and was about to rub her nose in it, even though I knew that was a traumatic and cruel thing to do after once seeing a group of cellar door customers do it to a wine-maker during a bad vintage.

'Stop!' yelled the kids. 'She's only obeying her genes. She's doing what her ancestors, the wolves, did on the tundra. She's marking out her territory.'

'Wolves on the tundra,' I said heatedly, 'did not make very expensive marble-effect kitchen floor tiles curl up at the edges. Besides, this isn't her territory, it's mine.'

The kids gave me a searching look. 'Then show her,' they said. 'Dogs are pack animals. They'll happily take a submissive role as long as they've got a leader to follow. Show her you're the leader of the pack.'

'Well,' I said to the dog later that evening, 'you're probably wondering why I've called this meeting. It's basically to examine the broad parameters of the urination issue, to give your input due consideration, and hopefully to reach a consensus.' The dog looked at me. Then she peed on her agenda papers.

I spent many hours staring into the mirror that night. I wasn't studying my external self, even though my knees were raw and my hands were chapped from sponging the carpet so much. I was looking into my soul. I was asking myself the most searching question a modern man can ask himself. Did I, a sensitive, non-aggressive, resource-sharing, gender-flexible person, have what it took to be a leader of the pack?

Did I even know what it took? Up till then I'd thought it took a Harley, a leather jacket and an underbite, but now I wasn't so sure. Did it involve burying food in unrefrigerated locations and digging it up several weeks later and eating it? Was sniffing my neighbours' genitals and then baring my teeth until they adopted a submissive posture a prerequisite? Would I have to pee on my own carpet?

As dawn's light revealed me huddled against the washing machine (I'd tried sleeping on the laundry floor but I hadn't even been able to manage that), I realised two things. One was that I was as much the product of my socialisation as the dog was of her genes. She'd always be a wolf and I'd always be a wimp.

The other was that when men in our suburbs gather together in animal skins and beat drums and wave spears, they're not struggling to be males, they're struggling to train dogs.

Actually, it's all worked out OK. The dog's taken over as leader of the pack. It means she can pee where she likes, but she also changes tap washers and decides when the car needs to go in for a service. It's a big weight off my mind. Now, if you'll excuse me, I've got to go and lie down on my back with my arms and legs in the air and whimper.

FEAR

I nearly pooped myself. It was brilliant.
*Customer at a theme park I once
fainted in*

*Animals use fear to avoid danger. Humans go in search of
it on bungy jumps, white-water rafting trips, mountain
climbs and honeymoons. I don't understand why one
group of mammals should behave so differently to all the
others. In fact I find it a bit scary.*

I WAS IN a bookshop recently and I picked up a book
called *Feel the Fear and Do It Anyway*. I put it straight
back down. One of my biggest fears is being caught
shoplifting.

It was a shame, because it might have helped me with
one of the other biggest fears in my life, changing the
headlight bulb in my car.

I know what you're thinking. A person's pretty

unlikely to have changing a headlight bulb as one of the biggest fears in their life. Actually, you're right, it's not one of my biggest fears, it's several of them.

The first fear was buying the new bulb. The spare parts shop is a foreign country to me and I don't speak the language. I envy my daughter, who did Auto Studies at school and can place an order for cow-pattern car seat covers without breaking into a sweat. Not me. I just point, which isn't very productive if all they have on the counter is an exchange muffler for a truck.

This time I felt the fear and did it anyway. I looked the counter bloke in the eye, shrugged off the nagging suspicion that real men go into their sheds with a bit of sand and wire and make their own headlight bulbs, resisted the temptation to point to the previous customer's cylinder head kit with gasket and cauliflower (he had all his shopping in the one bag) and asked for a headlight bulb.

I didn't actually use the words 'headlight bulb' because the stress of the moment made me forget them. What I actually asked for was 'one of those round things at the front of the car', but the bloke caught my drift when he handed me a wheel and I shook my head.

The next fear in the cluster emerged at home while I was taking the bulb out of the box to see why it had cost $32 when every other bulb I buy costs 95 cents, or $1.10 if it's more than 40 watts. Printed on the bulb was the word 'halogen', which I think is an abbreviation for 'handmade in the low-countries by genuine artisans'. Also printed on the bulb were the words 'do not touch the glass'. Anxiety jolted through me, more than 40 watts of it. I was already touching the glass. I put the bulb back into the box.

How was I going to insert the new bulb without touching the glass? I searched my car owner's manual for clues, half-dreading I'd find the words 'do not touch the page'. What I did find was a bulb-changing diagram of eye-watering complexity. I studied it and deciphered it, even though to do so I had to replace all the bulbs in my house with 100 watt ones.

Then I took a very deep breath and lifted the bonnet of the car. The screw-off rear panel of the headlight assembly was in approximately the place indicated by the diagram. What the diagram didn't indicate, however, didn't even hint at or give even the slightest health warning about, was that to unscrew the rear panel of the headlight assembly one had first to remove the car's battery.

I stared at the battery doubtfully, my head filling with fearful images. If I could remove the battery, if I could find the tools to loosen the battery-restraining assembly, what effect would battery-absence have on the rest of the car? I was dimly aware the car was controlled by a computer. Without power, would the computer's memory go middle-aged? When the battery was reconnected, would the computer go haywire and think it was the year 1900 and only allow the car to move if someone was walking in front with a red flag?

And how do you reconnect a car battery? I vaguely remember reading that if you reconnect the wrong terminal first, you electrocute yourself and melt the sun visors.

I reached for the owner's manual, then stopped, another fearful thought looming. I'm no expert, but the battery didn't look as though it would come out without someone first removing the alternator assembly. And to remove the alternator assembly-restraining assembly, it looked to me like the brake power-booster assembly would have to come out first. I closed my eyes. I also closed the bonnet.

Okay, I know I'm taking a risk. I know it's not sensible, driving at night with only one headlight. On an unlit road I could be mistaken for a motorbike. I could be attacked by a rival bikie gang. The risk terrifies me, but as the book says, feel the fear and do it anyway.

FORGETFULNESS

Forgetting is a purposeful act.
Sigmund Freud

For years I didn't understand what Freud meant by that, mostly because I couldn't remember exactly what he'd said. Then I remembered I'd jotted the words on the back of a dentist's appointment card. But where had I put it? I'd forgotten.

MY LIFE IS IN CHAOS. It's been that way for a while now. Six weeks probably, or perhaps four, or it could be nine. A while anyway, ever since I left my brain in a Los Angeles deli.

Not my grey squishy brain. I know I've still got that one because I can feel it hurting. The one I left in the deli was my real brain, the black plastic one. Or, to use the correct medical terminology, my Electronic Personal Organiser.

It was the grey squishy one's fault I was in the deli in the first place. One minute I was strolling along without a care in the world, idly trying to remember if smog can cause memory loss, the next the grey squishy one was demanding hot pastrami and a fudge sundae and sex with Michelle Pfeiffer.

That's the trouble with grey squishy brains, they're always making impossible demands. (Michelle Pfeiffer was on location in Tunisia and the deli only had banana smoothies.) Black plastic brains don't make impossible demands. All a black plastic brain ever needs is a new battery once a year. Or twice a year if you get banana smoothie in the battery compartment.

It was the grey squishy brain's fault I made the fateful phone call in the deli, too. The black plastic one beeped that it was time to finish and leave, but no, the grey squishy one insisted we go upstairs to the pay phone and ring my American publisher and see if my American book sales had improved in the three hours since I'd last asked.

They hadn't. My grey squishy brain got depressed for a while. Two hours probably, or perhaps three, or it could have been nine. My grey squishy brain had no way of knowing because, as it realised when it came to at the airport, it had left my black plastic brain sitting on the pay phone back in the deli.

I'll say this for my grey squishy brain. It didn't panic. Not at first. Even though it knew that most of the information I needed to get through the rest of my life was in the black plastic brain. Phone numbers. Deadlines. PIN numbers. My address.

Squishy stayed calm and formulated a three-stage recovery plan. (1) Taxi ride to deli. (2) Inspection of public phone. (3) Body search of customers, staff and all residents within a 10-kilometre radius.

Even when Squishy remembered that it was just minutes away from being loaded onto a plane back to Australia, it still didn't panic. Calmly it adjusted the recovery plan. (1) Phone call to deli. (2) Offer of large reward. (3) Pleading, sobbing and begging them to do the body searching.

Squishy only lost its cool when the assistant manager of the deli informed us that (1) my personal organiser was not on the pay phone, (2) it hadn't been handed in, and (3) there's a Californian law prohibiting body searches by people who handle chopped liver.

The panic attack was severe and lasted quite a while. Sixteen hours probably, or perhaps 18, or it could have been 36. The flight back to Australia was hell. I can't describe the feeling of leaving part of your brain behind in a foreign country. Now I know how people who fly back from Switzerland after serious cranial surgery must feel. And members of the Australian cricket team who fly home the day after victory drinks.

As soon as we landed I rushed to an automatic teller to withdraw cash to get change to ring a friend to ask her my PIN number. That's the trouble with grey squishy brains. They're great with impossible demands but hopeless with logical thought.

I found some coins in my bathroom bag and stuffed them into the phone. Then I discovered I couldn't remember any of my friends' phone numbers. That's the other trouble with grey squishy brains. They're great at thingummy point plans, but hopeless at remembering numbers.

I think at that point I must have had some kind of seizure. The next thing I knew I was lying on the arrivals hall carpet with a doctor bending over me explaining that it wasn't good to bang grey squishy brains on floors. I asked the doctor if there were any circumstances in which she would bang a patient's head on the floor. 'Certainly not,' she said. Then she discovered I couldn't remember my Medicare number.

I mustn't be too hard on Squishy. In the days or weeks or months since we've been back it's been under a lot of strain. To suddenly find you're flying solo again after five years with an autopilot is a shock. You find yourself regretting deeply that you didn't spend more time memorising birthdays, anniversaries and serial numbers and less time pondering the meaning of life and whether to have baked beans or fish fingers.

It's been a humbling experience, accepting that my birth brain is less effective and reliable than my sadly departed electronic one. I don't want to accept it, but each time I feel denial coming on I remind myself of the trouble I'm having remembering to go beep at ten past seven each morning.

So if anyone reading this has a fully programmed personal organiser they're finding a bit too new-fangled, I've got a pre-electronic brain in average condition for its age and I'd be happy to swap.

And if any of my friends are reading this, now you know why I haven't called. If you do get a call from someone with an American accent pretending to be me, could you ask him to look up my mother's phone number? He can ring it through to me here at home on 917 ... no, 719 ... hang on, it'll come to me ...

FORGIVENESS, LACK OF

I'll never forgive him for what he did, never. Not if he comes to me on his bended knees. Not even if he begs me. Not unless he buys me a dog.

Overheard on a bus

Experts suggest that if we forgive those who've deceived, betrayed, hurt and ridiculed us, we'll live happier lives and approach death with feelings of fulfilment and completion. But like all huge tasks, it needs to be attempted a step at a time. Start with small, manageable acts of forgiveness, they suggest, and leave the French till later.

I'M AS DETERMINED as ever to boycott French products. In fact I'm so determined I'm boycotting Belgian products as well, and any products from Liechtenstein used for serving Pernod.

I don't like doing it. I'd prefer a more constructive form of conflict resolution, such as saying to Mr Chirac that if he'll apologise for his nuclear policy in the Pacific we'll give him our Yoplait commercials.

But Mr Chirac seems resolute, and so we must be too. I've had plenty of practice. Within minutes of his announcement in 1995 that the tests were resuming I'd burnt the Eiffel Tower tea-towel, flushed away the Chanel No. 4 (I bought it in Bali – luckily it was very cheap), let the air out of the Michelin tyres and emptied the bottles of Evian water onto the kitchen curtains. (The flames had spread from the tea-towel.)

Then I went over to the neighbours and offered to drive their French poodle to an internment camp at Cowra. I told them if I couldn't find an internment camp I'd try and find a holiday kennel where the dogs at least had to make their own beds.

My offer wasn't warmly received. The neighbours threw me out and were fairly abusive. The exact words they used were '*allez*, imbecile', which I think must be French for 'How can you drive our dog to Cowra, you dickhead, when your tyres are folded up in the back of your wardrobe?'

They had a point, and their point was that boycotts are not easy, as I discovered when I began searching for Australian substitutes for my favourite French products.

Mineral water was the easiest. Ours looks the same, tastes the same and is 37 per cent cheaper. I'm just not sure, though, that ours has spent as many years filtering through as many sedimentary layers as the stuff from the French Alps. This occurred to me as I got back to the shopping centre car park. I tipped all six bottles out. I was parked on the top floor and in 2047 I'll take the empties down to the basement and catch the drips.

Cheese has been more difficult. It isn't the quality of ours that's the problem. Only last week I sampled a sublime pale orange rind-washed cheese from Western Victoria made from the milk of sheep that had been hand-fed Cheezels. Unforgettable. When it comes to brie, our own King Island can hold its mould cultures high among the fungi and microflora of the world. I've had a slice of it sitting on my cheese board for three weeks now and it looks as good as the French stuff in every regard. Unfortunately, though, I can't eat it because the Tasmanian government refuses to clarify in writing whether they do or do not have plans to conduct nuclear tests in Bass Strait.

It was while I was on the phone to the Tasmanian Department of Agriculture, Fisheries and Defence that an awful thought hit me. What of the less traditional French products? The ones whose labels are devoid of jolly gendarmes and funny marks over the vowels. Could we still be consuming those without even realising it?

I grabbed the nearest product at my place, which happened to be a skin moisturiser. (I'd been trying to soften up the rind of the Western Victorian cheese so I could eat that too.) The brand was a proudly Australian one, but what about the contents? I studied the list, keeping an eye out for anything with garlic in it.

Methylchloroisothiazolinone. Was that French? I tried saying it with a French accent. It sounded just the same as when I tried saying it with an Australian accent – three syllables and then lots of dribbling. I wrenched my mind back to French lessons at school. Had methylchloroiso-thiazolinone been on any of the vocab lists? It rang a bell, but then the French teacher had tended to slur his words.

While I was at the chemist's demanding to know the country of origin of all the ingredients in my moisturiser, another thought hit me. The chemist had just retorted by asking if I knew the country of origin of all the inks in the banknote I'd used to pay for the moisturiser, and I'd just said *touché*, which is French for touchy.

Mon Dieu, I thought, if we're doing this properly we should be boycotting French words as well. It's a daunting prospect. I don't even know what the English word for *cliché* is. The Aboriginal word is Canberra but overseas visitors can't be expected to know that.

What, for example, do we substitute for *enfant terrible*? 'Martin Amis, the toy-snatcher and projectile vomiter of the London literary scene' just doesn't have the same ring about it.

And what about *tête-à-tête*? I've tried, but I just can't invite friends round for a head-to-head. I don't know what worries me the most, that they won't come or that they'll bring hair transplant equipment.

It's hard, this boycott, because there's a little bit of France in all of us, and I don't just mean from the nuclear tests. Look at the patisseries in every shopping centre and the baguettes in every hot bread shop. Look at the way we cheerfully pay an extra $10 in a restaurant for a lump of meat if it's *en jus* instead of 'in its own blood'.

We respect things more when they're written in French. That's why those really expensive face creams are called masques. Don't tell anyone I said this, but if the tests start again my advice is to find an extra thick one, apply three layers and leave it on for the next 800 years. *Santé*.

GiVinG UP

Never. Bugger off.
The defenders of the Alamo

*I know history and self-help books are full of
inspirational examples of not giving up, but I'd just like
to say that I think giving up is perfectly OK in certain
circumstances. (1) When we're accepting the inevitability
of death. (2) When we're being tickled. (3) When we're on
the phone to the bank.*

SCENE ONE. My place. Day. Me on the phone to
the bank Home Loan Hotline. I don't know at the time
that later I'll be trying to reproduce the conversation
verbatim, so no recording equipment is in operation. The
following is seared pretty permanently into my brain,
however.

ME: Hello, do you do bridging finance?

BANK: Sorry?

ME: There's a house I'm hoping to buy, but I need a loan to cover the gap between buying it and selling my old house. Do you do that sort of loan?

BANK: Yes.

ME: Great. What's the interest rate please?

BANK: The standard variable rate is 9.25 per cent.

ME: OK. And I can have it for as short a time as I like?

BANK: Most people take it over 25 years.

ME: (Pause.) I think we've got a misunderstanding. I'm after a bridging loan.

BANK: A bridging loan.

ME: Yes. To tide me over till I can sell my house.

BANK: We can do it over 20 years.

ME: No, I'm sorry, you don't ...

BANK: How long do you need the loan for?

ME: I'm not sure exactly.

BANK: Ten years?

ME: No. You see ...

BANK: Five years?

ME: A few months. It depends how long my house takes to sell. Probably around three to six months.

BANK: We've got a fixed rate of 8.5 per cent.

ME: Oh, good.

BANK: That's for two years.

ME: For up to two years?

BANK: The loan period is two years.

ME: Or less.

BANK: No.

ME: (Pause.) That's not really bridging finance.

BANK: Are you purchasing an investment property?

ME: No, it's to live in.

BANK: We've got a special rate of 7.9 per cent.

ME: Good.

BANK: For the first 12 months.

ME: For up to 12 months?

BANK: No, you get the 7.9 per cent for the full 12 months.

ME: Can I get it for less than 12 months?

BANK: Less? (Long pause.) It's possible.

ME: (Hopeful.) Three months?

BANK: Yes.

ME: Or four months?

BANK: Yes.

ME: Perfect.

BANK: There would be an early repayment penalty of three months' interest.

ME: (Silence.)

BANK: Are you there sir?

ME: (Long pause.) Correct me if I'm wrong, but isn't the whole point of bridging finance that it's without early repayment penalties?

BANK: (Silence.)

ME: Open-ended?

BANK: (Silence.)

ME: Covering an unforeseen period of time?

BANK: You'll have to talk to your branch about that.

SCENE TWO. My place. Later the same day. Me on the phone to my branch loans officer.

ME: Hello, do you do bridging finance?

BANK: Yes.

ME: And that's where you lend me money so I can buy a new house and I pay you back when I sell my old house?

BANK: That's right.

ME: And the loan period is flexible?

BANK: Correct.

ME: To cover an unforeseen period of time?

BANK: Yes.

ME: And there are no early repayment penalties?

BANK: No.

ME: Wonderful. What's the interest rate?

BANK: How much do you need?

ME: (Pause.) I'm not sure exactly. Depends what I end up paying for the new house. And what I get for my place. And the interest rate. So as a guide, could you give me the rate for, say, a hundred thousand?

BANK: What's your date of birth?

ME: Sorry?

BANK: Your date of birth.

ME: Why?

BANK: For the application form.

ME: (Weakly.) No, listen, I don't want . . .

BANK: And I'll need your full name and address and the full name and address of any co-borrowers.

ME: (Feebly.) I just want . . .

BANK: And your gross annual incomes.

ME: I'm just inquiring about the interest rate. You don't need an application form for that, surely.

BANK: I'm sorry, sir, I do.

ME: Why?

BANK: Because we don't handle bridging loans at this branch and all referrals to head office have to be done in the form of an application.

ME: Can't you just tell me the interest rate?
BANK: I don't know it.
ME: Can I ring head office?
BANK: No need. They'll ring you.
ME: Why can't I ring them?
BANK: It's the way it's done.
ME: Why?
BANK: You'll have to speak to head office about that.

SCENE THREE. Bank head office. Days later. Nobody on the phone to me.

SCENE FOUR. My place. Weeks later. Me by the phone talking to myself.
ME: I didn't want to move house that much anyway. (Sigh.)

GRANDIOSITY

I am the greatest.
Muhammad Ali

For the rest of us, as we float like bees and sting like butterflies, humble is a much better option. But it's hard to achieve when the ten most used words in our language are stunning, fabulous, unique, sensational, brilliant, superb, magnificent, sublime, peerless and ravishing. And that's just about bathrooms in real estate ads. Perhaps we should follow Ali's example and remember that actions speak louder than words.

DO YOU EVER FANTASISE about doing something faster, slower, bigger, smaller, longer, shorter or with more house bricks between your teeth than anyone else and cracking a mention in *The Guinness Book of Records*? I do quite often. On March 27, 1995, I thought about it

6,249 times, which I'm pretty sure is a world record.

Unfortunately, I wasn't able to get my feat authenticated as my two independent witnesses failed to observe the correct procedure. After I'd mentioned getting in *The Guinness Book of Records* for the 138th time that morning they lost their tempers and locked me in a cupboard. I tried to point out that it was the 14th time they'd locked me in a cupboard that week which I was also pretty sure was a world record, but their only response was, 'Be quiet, Dad, we're not listening.'

When I shouted the exciting news to them – that they'd uttered those words 47,750 times in a 12-month period and were sure to be immortalised in *The Guinness Book of Records* – they stuck a hose through the keyhole and turned it on. Which illustrates my point. So powerful is the allure of The Book that the kids weren't content with breaking one record, they immediately wanted to start on another. (Unfortunately we weren't successful. The cold I caught from the hose had me sneezing for only 11 days, which was 966 days short of the record. They should have shut me in the fridge.)

Some people think that world records are only broken by aggressive type-A personalities, the sort of people who have no qualms about pushing themselves to the front of a 100-metre sprint or slicing a cucumber into 264 slices in 13.4 seconds and making an appalling mess in someone else's kitchen.

I disagree. I believe that deep in all of us, as we struggle to come to terms with mortality and 7 billion neighbours, the desire burns to leave a small but permanent mark on the world in a place that isn't a landfill.

Which is where *The Guinness Book of Records* comes in. With 70-odd million copies sitting on bookshelves and propping up wobbly settee legs around the world, it's hard to beat as a medium for immortality. (It's also hard to beat as a strategy for cracking a mention in itself. (1) Publish a book of world records. (2) Become the top-selling copyright book in publishing history. (3) Agree to accept your record for publication. Simple but brilliant.)

I've been trying to score a mention since I was 4½. (A record? Probably not. Sigh.) My early attempts fell woefully short of the mark. I thought I'd cracked it on my fifth birthday when I was allowed to stay up till eight o'clock, but that same night a kid in my street broke the 8.15 barrier by faking St Vitus's dance.

Undeterred, I threw myself into other record attempts. For a while I became obsessed with plate spinning, until my mother pointed out that record-breaking plate spinners always finished their dinner and washed them up first.

The closest I ever came to making it into The Book was the momentous day I packed 102 Smarties into my mouth at once. The record wasn't allowed to stand because I refused to spit them out for verification. Stupid, I know, but I went through a stubborn phase in my 30s.

The problem for us would-be immortals, I've realised, is that all the good records have been set. How I yearn for innocent days long-gone when wellie throwing, beer-mat flipping, cigar-box balancing and haggis hurling were uncharted fields of human endeavour.

And most of the records are already unbeatable. Records that involve doing something for ages and ages, for example. The simple fact is that the human organism, whether we're cracking jokes, making omelettes or manhandling a fire pump, can stay awake for no more than about 70 hours, 90 if we're firewalking.

Which is why I've decided to turn my back on The Book and its traditional records and attempt some new feats that have more relevance to contemporary life. The other day, for example, in a 45-minute car journey across an Australian city, I stopped at 63 sets of traffic lights. If anyone can beat that, please let me know. (I should be fair and mention that some of them were green.) I'm also interested to hear from anyone who's been crashed into from behind by more than 16 vehicles in a single trip.

Last week I was in a packed 200-seat inner-city restaurant and was the only customer not wearing black. Hard to believe, I know, but two independent adult witnesses of standing in the community verified that during the three minutes I was there, not one other cus- tomer arrived naked. (I only got one of the witnesses' names. It was Constable Whelan.)

For me, though, the really exciting records of the future will be achieved not in the physical world, but in the mind. I'm planning to hire a virtual-reality helmet and a PR company. That way I can spend a comfortable half-hour at home and have both myself and the media believing it was 78 hours in a shopping centre with a wheelbarrow on my head.

Wait a sec, forget all that. I've just had a call from *The Guinness Book of Records*. They've heard I'm writing a chapter about *The Guinness Book of Records* and they've just said that if I mention *The Guinness Book of Records* four times in the last paragraph, they'll put me in *The Guinness Book of Records* in a brand new category (Author – Most Mentions In A Single Chapter Of A Book He Didn't Write).

GREED

Greed is good.

Someone in an 80s movie

I'm still not sure who it was because I'd bought the ultra-large popcorn and I couldn't see the screen. Anyway, he was a wimp. He didn't know the first thing about greed. He thought it was all about money.

CHRISTMAS IS OVER, the Quick-Eze have all been consumed (I find indigestion tablets are more popular in my Christmas pudding than sixpences), the inappropriate presents have all been returned to the pet shop, and it's time to make some New Year resolutions.

I've made mine already.

1. On my next Christmas list, specify that the frogs be chocolate.
2. Read more books.

Those of you who've seen my resolutions in past years (I usually paint them on the side of the house so I don't forget them) will know that (2) is a regular. I've been trying to read more books for about eight years now and, until this year, failing miserably.

Each year, despite (2), my book consumption has dwindled. I've been taking longer and longer to finish a book, and not just the big ones such as *War and Peace* and the Calcutta White Pages. Slim volumes have taken me weeks. Months if they were written by physicists in wheelchairs.

I've racked my brains to work out why. I thought it might have been my eyesight, but I went to the optometrist and read the chart perfectly, and in only three hours.

The kids suggested that perhaps subtle changes in my brain chemistry were affecting the way I process written information. 'That can happen,' they said, 'with the onset of senile dementia.'

The awful thought occurred to me that perhaps I didn't like books anymore. That after a lifetime of book passion I was developing a subconscious hankering for crocheting or dog breeding. I knew that couldn't be right. Bookshops were still my favourite places after stationery shops and chocolate-frog processing plants. I was still buying huge numbers of books. My bedside table still looked like the CBD.

A few months ago I became so desperate I went out and bought every book on the subject I could find. I started reading one immediately. *Women Who Read Too Much, Men Who Read Too Little* it's called and it's very interesting. Well, the first part of chapter one is.

But it didn't really address my problem. The problem of a normal healthy man with a normal healthy appetite for books who found he was reading less and less each year, and not just because his bedside table was blocking out the light.

Then last week, while I was jotting down my New Year resolutions, it hit me. I got so excited I almost fell off the ladder at the side of the house. Time, I realised, that's the problem. We've sped up time. Our lives don't go at book speed these days, they go at microwave, DVD, instant-stain-removal, eight-valves-per-cylinder, just-add-hot-water-and-stir speed.

I looked at my life and asked myself when I'd last had an unbroken 10 hours for any activity other than cleaning the fridge. (And even then most of that time was spent trying to free my head from the meat compartment.)

I couldn't remember.

Okay, I said to myself, if I can't slow my life down to book speed, I'll just have to speed up my reading.

The next day I investigated speed-reading courses. There were heaps available, but the depressing thing was how long they all took. Weeks, some of them. Months if they were run by physicists in wheelchairs.

Then I found what I was looking for. A speed speed-reading course. Two hours including the trip to the bank to pay for it. It's changed my life.

So far this year I've read 87 books including lots I've been meaning to read for ages. *A Suitable Boy* by Vikram Seth for example, which turns out to be a charming novella about a bloke having a quick walk down a street somewhere dusty. Pakistan I think, or perhaps Bourke.

And David Marr's superb biography of Patrick White. Isn't it incredible how many great novels that man was able to produce given that he only lived for three-and-a-half years?

And I really enjoyed Jackie Collins' new one. I didn't actually catch the title but there were some wonderful sex scenes. I think they were sex scenes. They might have been shopping scenes but they were wonderful anyway.

What I've discovered over the past four days is that while speed is an important part of reading more books, so is grabbing every opportunity. I shudder now to think of how much reading time I was letting slip away each day, each hour, each minute.

In the car, for example, there are endless opportunities to take in a quick chapter. Between gear changes, or on any straight stretch longer than eight metres, and certainly while braking. I read Samuel J. Kant's *The Subjectivity Of Colour* at a red light. Well, most of it. I couldn't finish all the footnotes because it turned out the light was green.

So far this year I haven't experienced a single pang of guilt about my book consumption. I read in the shower, during phone conversations and while I'm cooking dinner. I've even devised a way of consuming books while I'm asleep, and expect to have Proust finished by the middle of next week if the kids' voices last.

There's only one problem, only one thing missing from my otherwise rich and full and satisfying life. There's no time to watch telly.

GUILT

Ah, guilt, the champagne of neuroses.
*Me, but I think
I stole it from someone.
Sorry.*

*If humans stopped experiencing guilt, the bottom
would fall out of the sleeping-pill market overnight.
Drug companies would have to get by selling aspirin.
And poison. And explosives. So next time it's 3 a.m.
and you're in the grip of the Big G, remember one thing.
You might not be getting much sleep, but at least
you're helping keep society intact.*

TUESDAY 9.46 P.M. Put out garbage. Place six plastic
yogurt containers, two Irish stew tins, one antacid bottle
and one cookbook in bin. Receive disapproving look
from neighbour. Notice that most other houses in street
have recycling bins. Feel guilty.

WEDNESDAY 10.15 A.M. Ring the local council.

ME: Hello, I've just moved into the area and I don't have a recycling bin. Could I have one delivered please?

COUNCIL OFFICER: Sorry, we don't deliver recycling bins.

ME: Oh. Not even when you come round to empty the existing recycling bins?

COUNCIL OFFICER: No.

ME: Oh. Why not?

COUNCIL OFFICER: Too expensive. We're losing money on the bins as it is, giving them away.

ME: But surely recycling lowers your other waste disposal costs. I'd have thought you would be encouraging residents to recycle, not making it harder.

COUNCIL OFFICER: We do encourage recycling. Very much so. In fact, the council has a very pro-active recycling policy.

ME: So how do I get a bin?

COUNCIL OFFICER: You'll have to come and pick one up.

THURSDAY 2:30 P.M. Drive to council offices. Step into lavish foyer. Think for a second I've wandered into Hyatt by mistake. See council recycling poster on wall. Phew.

RECEPTIONIST: Can I help you?

ME: I'd like a recycling bin please.

RECEPTIONIST: We don't have recycling bins here.

ME: They're round the back, are they?

RECEPTIONIST: No, they're at our waste management depot.

ME: Next door?

RECEPTIONIST: No, it's about 10 kilometres away.

ME: Oh.

RECEPTIONIST: It's open till four, and if you can't make it by then, our construction and maintenance depot across the road from it has recycling bins too.

ME: Thanks.

3 P.M. Set out for the council waste management depot. Heavy traffic.

3.20 P.M. Approach depot street. Discover end of street cut off by freeway built since my edition of street directory published. Shrug and laugh.

3.21 P.M. Heavy traffic.

3.35 P.M. Approach other end of street. Discover other end of street cut off by light rail built since my edition of street directory published.

3.36 P.M. Heavy traffic.

3.45 P.M. Approach depot by side street. Discover side street now a flyover built since my edition etc. Swear at street directory. Tell it that as soon as we get home I'm throwing it out. Remember I haven't got a recycling bin.

3.55 P.M. Find another side street. Drive as fast as is legally permissible towards depot. Experience stress pains in stomach. Wonder if waste management depot has facilities for disposal of ruptured spleen.

3.59 P.M. Arrive at depot. One minute to spare. Park right outside. Congratulate self on good fortune. Leap out of car and sprint to gate. Gate locked. Depot closed. Sign says 9 a.m. to 3.30 p.m. Stare in disbelief. Rattle gate. Experience abdominal cramps. Take deep breaths and calm down. Remind self that ruptured spleen now can't be disposed of until 9 a.m. tomorrow.

4.01 P.M. Remember receptionist's advice re construction and maintenance depot across road.

4.03 P.M. Arrive at construction and maintenance depot. Place deserted. Poke head into offices and demountable huts. No people. No recycling bins. One metal waste-paper bin, but full of waste paper. Bloke in overalls turns corner and stops, startled to see me.

ME: G'day. I'm after a recycling bin.

BLOKE: A what?

ME: A recycling bin. Do you have any of them here?

BLOKE: Nah.

ME: I was told I could get one here.

BLOKE: Nah. Waste management depot across the road.

ME: They're closed.

BLOKE: Yeah. You'll have to come back tomorrow.

ME: Do you have somewhere I can dispose of a ruptured spleen? (Didn't actually say this but could have if I'd had a couple more minutes to think.)

4.15 P.M. Drive home. Heavy traffic. Prepare evening meal using only ingredients from non-recyclable containers. Least successful casserole ever. But then I've never liked potato chips or wine gums much.

FRIDAY 9.45 A.M. Drive back to council waste management depot. Find it first time thanks to trail of torn street directory pages. Fill out lengthy form. Receive recycling bin. Weep briefly.

10.30 A.M. Drive home. Use idling periods to try to calculate how many times recycling bin will need to be filled to offset volume of fossil fuel used to get recycling bin.

11.40 A.M. Proudly position recycling bin in front yard. Place in it first object to be recycled. Copy of council recycling policy. See something in bushes. Old recycling bin with my house number painted on it.

11.45 A.M. Pick up phone to ring council with inquiry about recycling recycling bins. Experience tummy pain.

TUESDAY 9.46 P.M. Put out garbage. Stuff old recycling bin into wheelie bin. Disapproving look from neighbour. Feel guilty.

WEDNESDAY 10.15 A.M. Etc.

hASTE

Beep beep.
The Roadrunner

Serenity and bliss, we are told, come from emulating the ancient mystics who lived completely in the moment, sometimes for decades. Very difficult for us westerners whose only mountain-dwelling role-model is a bird on steroids. Ah well, at least we have holidays.

THE CROWD stood hushed as the tour guide's voice rang through the vast crypt. 'Napoleon's Tomb is sacred to the French people,' he said, 'and every year hundreds of thousands of them make a pilgrimage here to contemplate the Emperor's mighty deeds, some with reverence, some with pride, but very few of them, monsieur, with a frying pan.'

I realised with a start he was looking at me. His gaze

became a scowl as he regarded the Escargots à la Mode de Jardin bubbling away on my camping stove. 'Sorry,' I said, 'I know it's rude to cook while you're talking, but I'm a bit pushed for time. I've only got three minutes for lunch. As it is I'll have to have the snails rare.'

As it was I didn't get to have the snails at all. I tried to explain to the security guards as they marched me out how hungry this would leave me, given that afternoon tea wasn't until 4.17 and even then I probably wouldn't be able to eat much in the 25 seconds I'd scheduled.

They didn't listen. Nor did they listen when I tried to explain the pressure I was under. 'It's all right for you,' I said, 'you live here. You can see Paris any time, except during heavy smog. I'm an Australian. It takes me 24 hours to get here, three days to recover from the flight and two weeks in a language school before I can start seeing the sights. Which unfortunately only leaves one day so if you wouldn't mind, could you boot me out in the direction of the Eiffel Tower. I'm due there at 1.03.'

Thank God for Le Métro. I doubt if there's an underground rail system anywhere in the world that's better at transporting large numbers of passengers so speedily and efficiently. Also it keeps people off the streets so they don't block the path of Australian tourists sprinting to the next sight.

The lift operator at the Eiffel Tower was almost as unsympathetic as the tour guide at Napoleon's Tomb. True, he let me wedge the lift doors open with my exhausted body so I could view some of the other sights through my binoculars on the way up. But when I asked him to ring the Louvre and get them to open a window so I could have a squiz at the *Mona Lisa*, he pretended to be deaf. I knew he wasn't, though, because when I asked him if he had any Impressionist tattoos I could look at to save me a trip to the Musée d'Orsay, he punched me. A woman shrieked and fainted, which saved me a trip to L'Opéra.

Which was just as well because I needed to make a phone call. I knew French bureaucracy could be slow, but I never dreamed a call to the Mayor of Paris suggesting he tarmac all the roads because cobblestones are hopeless for roller skates could take nearly four minutes. Then again he did know a lot of swearwords.

I was almost late getting to the Champs Elysées. There was a traffic jam in the Place Charles de Gaulle which held me up for nearly three minutes. I thought it was going to be longer what with all the trucks blocking the road and the demolition contractors milling around asking who'd booked them to shift the Arc de Triomphe and put it next to the Cathedral of Notre Dame.

It was in Notre Dame that I was stopped in my tracks by an old priest. He was perched serenely on a bench gazing up at a stained-glass window. 'Is it not better to spend a day seeing one thing, my son,' he said, 'than to spend a day looking at a hundred things and not ...' (I'm afraid I missed the last few words. It was 3.28 and I was due at the Luxembourg Gardens.)

Seventeen minutes later I stopped for a coffee. (It would have been earlier but between the Bois de Boulogne and the Pompidou Centre I forgot to tip the madame concierge in a public toilet and was held in an arm-lock for 11 seconds.)

This was actually my 38th coffee of the day. That's the great thing about coffee in Paris. No need to sit down and mess around with coffee pots and fancy biscuits. Just slap some coins on a bar and slug it down. Unfortunately, though, it is quite strong and the unwary can be caught unawares.

'You're nicked,' said the two gendarmes, catching me unawares.

'Eh?' I said, with the distracted air of one who's due at the Place de la Concorde in nine seconds.

'We've been following you all day,' they said, nodding at a police car with smoking tyres, 'and we've clocked you travelling over the speed limit 38 times. We'd have booked you earlier, but we were trying to work out how you were doing it without a car.'

'It's the coffee,' I explained, 'and the fact that I'm an Australian tourist.'

They were unmoved. They started filling out forms.

'Come on,' I said, 'get a move on. I've got 25 bridges to wander dreamily over and I've only got two seconds for each of them as it is.'

The forms turned out to be speeding fines. I added them up while climbing the Montparnasse tower (the lift was too slow so I took the stairs), converted the total to a more familiar currency in the Place des Vosges (pausing only to give the concierge at the Palais Royal the name of a good escalator company), and by the time I'd let my fingers do the walking along the Rue de Rivoli (my feet were killing me) I'd come up with the title of my next book: *Europe on $19,000 a Day*.

iGNORAnCE

You'll never never know if you never never go.
Daryl Somers

Clever Northern Territory Tourist Authority. They know all about one of our deepest fears. That in the information age, ignorance isn't bliss, it's a shameful affliction. (Don't feel bad. I didn't know that either until recently.)

THE REPAIRMAN peered into my clothes dryer, frowned, had a huddled conversation with his accountant, rang his travel agent to check the cost of a skiing holiday in New Zealand, then gave me the bad news.

'It needs a new thermostat regulator,' he said, 'and the Saab, sorry solenoid, needs replacing. Plus there's a stress fracture in the air duct, but they don't make them separately so I'll have to fit a whole new exhaust outlet assembly.'

I tried to ask him how much all this would cost, but my own air duct seemed to be experiencing a stress fracture too. The repairman anticipated my question.

'Including the $90 you've already spent on the service call and quote, he said, fingers dancing over his calculator, 'that will come to $279.'

I should have anticipated his answer, the price of a new dryer being $289. We looked at each other for a long moment, the silence broken only by the distant sound of his apprentice out in the van buying a time-share in Bermuda.

My thoughts whirled around like the underwear of a person with $279. Was I being ripped off? Would the thermostat regulator have been fine with a squirt of oil and a wipe down with a damp pair of underpants? Did clothes dryers even have solenoids, or were solenoids only found in heavy earth-moving equipment and characters in *Star Trek*?

It was at that moment I finally had to admit the shameful truth. I'm an educated and fairly intelligent person who's spent more than four decades roaming the planet absorbing information and I still don't know how most things in my life work.

The toaster goes on the blink and I spend hours poring over manuals and circuit diagrams, only to give up in frustration without even being able to find the rubber band that makes the toast pop up.

Cars are a nightmare. I've spent a big part of my life gripping steering wheels in a cold sweat, trying to work out if the clunking I can hear is coming from the suspension, the transmission or that bit up the front I should never have unscrewed to try to clean. (The engine.)

I shudder when I remember the first time the kids asked me where the picture goes when you turn the telly off. I gave them a long, complex, scientific answer, only to have them expose an embarrassing gap in my knowledge. 'No, Dad,' they said wearily, 'it doesn't go next door, we've checked.'

I've tried to become more knowledgeable, I really have. I never go anywhere without a screwdriver, and I'm often to be seen at dinner parties and soirees dismantling something to see what makes it tick. I'm now intimate with the inside of a fanforced oven for example, after one recent hostess shut me in hers for most of the evening. I thought she over-reacted a bit. All I did was wonder aloud how her husband's pacemaker worked.

It's not ignorance itself that's so hard to live with, it's the fear that results from it. If I don't know exactly how my watch works (and I don't, even though I've had it apart six times) how can I be sure it's telling the right time? I can ask other people, but what if they don't know how their watches work? Really know, I mean, not vague notions about quartz vibrating at the same speed as the talking clock.

Suddenly we're faced with a nightmare scenario of sundials and missed appointments. Important appointments in some cases. The man who puts my watch back together doesn't like to be kept waiting.

I don't know about you, but sometimes my fear becomes too much to bear.

'Please,' I begged a member of the cabin crew on a flight recently, 'explain how a plane works.'

She frowned at me. 'Which bit of a plane?' she asked.

'The engines,' I replied, '. . . and the parachutes.'

'The engines are simple,' she said. 'Jet propulsion involves the rapid displacement of large volumes of air. It's the second law of aerodynamics.'

I felt my panic rising. 'What's the first law?' I asked.

What if she didn't know? What if the pilot didn't know?

The flight attendant sighed. 'The first law of aerodynamics states that if a passenger doesn't get up off his knees and stop hugging my shins, he'll spend the rest of the flight in the baggage hold.'

I got up. 'Okay,' I said, 'back to the second law. I still don't understand how a jet engine works.'

The attendant sighed again. 'It's very simple,' she said. 'The plane moves through the sky instead of dropping like a stone because in each engine is a revolving drum sucking air through itself. It's just like your clothes dryer at home.'

I fainted.

Back home, I was still feeling a bit wobbly when the dryer repairman whipped out his calculator and gave me the bad news. Wobbly, but still capable of taking decisive action without dribbling.

'Enough,' I said. 'From this moment on let my life be free of technology I don't understand. Take my video. Take my fridge. Take my fridge magnets. Forget the dryer, I'll get a clothes line. And put that calculator away and give me a simple, honest figure for your service call.'

'Righto,' said the repairman, licking the stub of a pencil and scribbling on the back of an envelope. 'Service call, quote and manual account preparation, $279.'

IMPATIENCE

Ommmmmmmmmmmmmmm.
Very patient person

*What hope did our species ever have of developing
patience? Nine whole months hanging round waiting to
be born. Hours getting out. An extra 45 minutes in the
car on the way home because Dad got lost trying to buy
cigars. Is it any wonder that the universal cry of the
impatient person is 'I'll do it myself'?*

I USED TO THINK the most terrifying words in the world
were 'war', 'death' and 'excuse me, sir, I'll have to ask
you to accompany me back into the store because you
haven't paid for that lingerie you're wearing under your
suit'.

Then I discovered assemble-it-yourself furniture. 'Insert
Allen key A into socket B and slide towards securing

device C exposing flaps D and E while taking care not to disengage tension trusses F and G or dislocate reinforcing plate H.' And that was just opening the carton.

I don't know who Allen was, but his key has brought misery to my life and very painful chafing to my fingertips. Why can't AIY furniture employ a more user-friendly method of assembly? Would it really increase the price of a wardrobe that much to include a rivet gun?

Last week I bought a new office chair. I've needed one for ages because my old chair just hasn't been giving me the lower-back support I've required since I dislocated my coccyx assembling it.

The people in the shop assured me the new chair would be much easier to put together. 'A child can do it,' they said. I asked if the child was available, but they didn't hear because my vertebrae were squeaking too loudly.

At home I unpacked the chair parts and studied the instruction sheet. It was covered with blurred and wobbly diagrams. My first impulse was to panic, but instead I persevered and 50 minutes later – success! I'd worked out which way up the instruction sheet was meant to go.

An hour later I had the castors inserted into the legs, the seat post inserted into the seat post cover and the base plate adjustment screw inserted into an envelope with a stiff letter to the manufacturer. The letter pointed out that adjustment screw E was a different size from adjustment socket F. Actually I used F to describe the adjustment screw as well, and the instruction sheet, the chair and their company.

Don't get me wrong. I can see that AIY furniture is a

boon to a great many people. The way it packs into flat, manageable cartons that fit into car boots. And behind fridges when you give up trying to assemble it and never want to see it again.

Many people do succeed in assembling it, of course, or the AIY furniture stores would have long ago been disassembled and packed into flat, manageable cartons. For those lucky Allen key virtuosos, most of whom I suspect are called Allen, the satisfaction must be immense. In a complex, baffling world where most of us comprehend so little so much of the time, to start off with a dozen pieces of timber and end up with a CD tower must be a joy, even if you had hoped for a bed.

But I do worry that in assembling our own furniture we may be disassembling the very structure of our society. Families are held together by their own histories. Will future generations feel the same way about their traditions when their family heirlooms can be reduced to a pile of chipboard planks? (Assuming, of course, they also inherited the Allen key and the instruction sheets.)

And what about relationships? Will couples survive bitter arguments now that they can have the entire contents of the house in the boots of their cars in less time than it takes to apologise? Perhaps we owe more to glued furniture than we've ever realised. I know several marriages that have survived mostly because the settee wouldn't fit into the hatchback.

I also worry about the effect AIY furniture is having on our intellectual lives. I don't have dinner parties any more mostly because I can't get the legs to stay on my dining table. Friends who do are increasingly telling me the same thing. Guests' conversation is either about constructing bookshelves, desks and entertainment centres or deconstructing books, plays and films. There has to be a connection.

Me, I'm just pleased I've solved the adjustment screw E problem. I'd confused adjustment socket F with frustrated screwdriver stab hole G. Plus I've worked out why my office chair diagrams are so hard to read. The designer had to do them standing up because he didn't know how to put his office chair together.

Well, I'm doing better than him. My old chair's in the garbage and I'm sitting at my desk and my lower back pain has almost gone. Who'd have thought an assemble-it-yourself chair carton could be so comfortable?

IMPRACTICALITY

**Ah, but a man's reach should exceed his grasp,
Or what's a heaven for?**
Robert Browning

*Self-help books are divided on the question of practicality.
Some advise us to keep our feet on the ground and our
hands firmly on our electronic organisers. Others exhort us
to take fearless leaps outside our zones of comfort and
proven competence. If only they warned us not to do it
when the children are watching.*

I'VE HAD QUITE a few powerful emotional experiences
at the movies. The first time I saw *Citizen Kane*, for
example, and realised that if you shake one of those
Perspex bubbles you get snow.

When I saw *Shine* my life was changed forever.
I stumbled out of the cinema, head ringing and heart
pounding. 'We feel the same,' said the kids. 'It's the three
choc-tops and the large Coke.'

But it wasn't just sugar coursing through my veins, it was inspiration. 'I've just seen my destiny,' I told them.

They looked at me, concerned. 'Mental illness?' they asked.

'No,' I replied. 'I now realise I was born to make music.'

The kids wept and pleaded. They showed me glossy brochures of incredibly well-appointed and luxurious psychiatric hospitals.

'It's no good,' I said sternly. 'I can't be tempted. Not even if those electric shock machines do get Foxtel. Music is my life now.'

The kids started kneading wax crayons into small, soft, ear-sized lumps. 'But, Dad,' they said desperately, 'you already make music. On your xylophone.'

I smiled at them. They meant well, but how could they know the passions that were stirring within me? Sure, I'd spent many hundreds of happy hours with my xylophone, but suddenly it wasn't enough.

I tried to explain. 'A musician just can't achieve a mystical creative bond with his instrument,' I told them, 'when it's actually being played by a fluffy pink battery-operated rabbit.'

I went to a music shop to choose a new instrument. My first choice was a piano. I sat at one and communed. It was a superb concert grand and I felt inspiration welling up inside me. But something wasn't quite right. I knew in my guts just how I wanted to play the Rachmaninoff, but try as I did I just couldn't achieve it on that piano. I think my romantic muse was intimidated by the $20,000 price tag. Plus the lid was locked.

I went over to the clarinet section and picked one up.

It was smaller than I'd imagined, and now I had it in my hands it didn't seem anything like as complicated. I put it to my lips, tried to remember the advice I'd read from the jazz greats, and played. At first I had some trouble finding that direct conduit between the soul and the instrument. Then I remembered I was meant to be blowing not sucking.

'Not bad for a first-timer, eh?' I said to the sales assistant. 'I reckon the clarinet's a piece of cake. Beats me why Mozart didn't ever manage to play one.'

The assistant sighed. 'That's just a reed, sir,' he said. 'The clarinet's over there.' He pointed to something with about 16 holes and 42 levers.

I considered a violin for a while, but the one in the shop had a serious design fault exactly like my telephone. I've never been able to hold that between my chin and my shoulder either.

Then, just as I was trying to choose between a tambourine and a triangle, a wondrous sound filled the shop. It was a child, playing golden notes on a small silver instrument. 'At last,' I cried. 'My musical destiny. My parents were always getting me to blow into the exhaust pipe of the car to clear out the rust. I should have realised I was destined to play the flute.'

The sales assistant sighed again. 'It's a harmonica,' he said.

I bought one and rushed home and started to play. Simple stuff at first. Blues riffs. Sea shanties. Bits from old Clint Eastwood movies. I thought the sea shanties were particularly evocative.

Others in the house thought so too. While I was playing, I saw cockroaches in the kitchen dancing a hornpipe. You know, the traditional nautical dance where the dancers lie on their backs and kick their legs in the air.

'Dad,' yelled the kids, 'there's something wrong with that harmonica. It doesn't sound right.' I frowned and checked that I'd remembered to take it out of the box. The kids played a scale. 'See,' they said. 'Several of the notes are bung.'

I frowned. 'Are they?' I said.

Back in the shop the sales assistant frowned too. 'Are you sure?' he said.

'No,' I said, 'but the kids do music at school.'

The assistant peered into the harmonica. 'Play a scale,' he said.

'I can't,' I said, 'not in the right order, and the kids are at home having their rooms soundproofed.'

The assistant took the harmonica and held it against a velvet box with a handle at the front and a hand-pump at the back. He pumped air through it. All the notes sounded bung. 'Frigging thing,' he muttered. I wondered if I should offer to go and get my fluffy pink rabbit.

'Why don't *you* play a scale?' I asked the assistant.

'Because,' he said, 'the health department won't allow it.'

For a while I thought he must have been such a loud player that his workmates' hearing would be at risk. Then I realised he was talking about mouth germs.

'Well, you'll just have to trust me,' I said, 'and replace it.'

The assistant shook his head. 'Sorry,' he said, 'we can't replace harmonicas. The health department won't let us. I'll have to send it back to the manufacturer.'

I stared at him. 'How will they test it,' I asked, 'if they're not allowed to play it and those little squeeze-boxes don't work?'

The assistant shrugged. 'Dunno,' he said.

My head started to spin and I realised *Shine* wasn't such a great movie after all. How could it be when they'd left out the most important scene? The one where David Helfgott has his first experience of mental derangement shortly after buying a harmonica.

iNCOMPETEnCE

In a hierarchy every employee named Peter tends to rise to his level of incompetence.

Laurence J. Peter and Raymond Hull,
The Peter Principle
(paraphrased)

As does, I fear, every human being in a loving relationship. What could be more natural than wanting to surpass a loved one's expectations? To push oneself to the absolute limits of one's physical, intellectual and emotional capacities, and beyond? Into parenthood.

THERE COMES A TIME in every father's life when his kids climb on to his knee and gaze trustingly into his eyes and ask him for certain information, with diagrams if possible.

My turn came last week. I thought I was prepared. I'd read biology textbooks, safe-sex pamphlets and an illustrated history of the rubber industry. I'd swotted up on the reproductive habits of mammals, amphibians, insects and the royal family. I was quietly confident.

'Dad . . .' said my daughter. She paused and wrinkled her brow. I could see this was more difficult for her than for me.

'Don't worry,' I said, patting her arm, 'I know what you want to ask. The answer is that it's perfectly okay as long as both parties are consenting adults and they love each other and the curtains are drawn.'

My daughter looked blank.

'If they're amphibians or insects,' I went on, 'they probably don't have to worry about the curtains.'

She still looked blank. I realised I may have jumped the gun. 'Sorry,' I said. 'I thought you wanted to know about kissing.'

She rolled her eyes. I could see I was making things worse.

'Please,' I said, 'ask me anything you want, without fear or embarrassment, and I promise I'll give you a straight answer.'

'Okay,' she said. 'Have you made adequate financial provision for your retirement?'

It was my turn to look blank. What did this have to do with biology? Was she concerned I might not be able to afford future editions of the textbooks? I was confused. Plus I was getting cramp in my tendons. A teenage daughter can be quite a strain on an ageing knee, particularly when her boyfriend's sitting next to her.

'We're just concerned,' said the boyfriend, 'that with your retirement little more than 20 years away, you may not be building your asset base to a realistic level. Financial planning experts warn that retiring with a lump-sum of less than 10 times your final year's income can result in a tragically degraded lifestyle and frayed cuffs.'

'Particularly,' said my daughter, 'for people with expensive tastes in magazines with royal sex scandals on the cover.'

I moved quickly to put their minds at rest. First, I showed them my extensive cash reserves. Well, I didn't actually show them because I didn't want to have to smash the piggy bank, but I rattled it.

'There are some very rare coins in here,' I said, 'including a gold doubloon.'

The boyfriend was impressed. 'Hapsburg?' he asked.

'Darrell Lea,' I replied, 'but it's a few years old so it should be worth a bit if the chocolate hasn't melted.'

The young folk looked doubtful. Rather than quibble, I showed them the rest of my portfolio of collectables. 'Antiquarian books are fetching top prices in the auction rooms,' I said.

My daughter nodded. 'Unfortunately, though,' she said, 'antiquarian copies of Mills & Boon aren't among them.'

'All right,' I said, opening my safe and carefully removing several layers of tissue paper. 'This'll stop you worrying. Antique snuff boxes. A collection exactly this size and vintage sold recently at Sotheby's for half a million dollars.'

The young folk stared.

'Half a million dollars,' they said, 'for a pile of the wooden crates snuff factories used to pack their product in? That's unbelievable.'

Okay, perhaps I had overestimated the worth of my snuff boxes. And my stamps. (I thought rubber ones would be more valuable than paper ones.) And my Louis XIV writing desk, though I still think the 14 photos of

Louis Armstrong under the Estapol make it unique and desirable.

'It's what we feared,' sighed my daughter. 'You're another baby boomer who's coasted too long on the privileges of your generation and now you'll be looking to us to subsidise your retirement home and *New Idea* subscription.'

I deeply resented that. For a start, I hate being referred to as a baby boomer. It's not my fault I had excessive wind as a new-born. Plus, I am absolutely determined I will never be a financial burden to anybody with the possible exception of Bill Gates if I can get his phone number.

I told the young folk so, and set about putting my financial affairs in order. First, I investigated super-annuation. It wasn't a happy option. Taking into account taxes, possible negative returns and too few investment years, I calculated I could achieve the retirement sum I needed but only if each year between now and retirement I contributed slightly more than my annual income.

I scoured the financial pages for a high-return, low-risk, sure-thing, absolutely guaranteed retirement-sustaining investment. Nothing. Or that's what I thought until I finally saw it. The one financial opportunity too good to ignore. The best ride on the whole fiscal merry-go-round.

I spotted it while I was perusing the bank interest rates on cash deposits. Yes, I thought, of course, that's it. A ready-made retirement-fund strategy. It doesn't involve buying shares, debentures, futures contracts, bonds, unit trusts, annuities or real estate. It just involves becoming a bank.

I'm planning to start right away. Then I too can pay

interest of 0.5 per cent on amounts less than $10,000 and charge 9.5 per cent on personal loans and 11.5 per cent on overdrafts. Okay, there'll be overheads, but I'm not greedy. I'll only need one branch and I should be able to cash-flow that out of a 1,600 per cent profit margin.

Phew, that's a relief. For me and for the young folk. Three cheers for financial deregulation, eh?

iNSECUR/ty

Which bank?
Advertisement

A wise old security guard once told me that insecurity is just a form of identity crisis. This helpful insight has served me well over the years. Whenever I feel insecure, I remember that I'm merely losing sight of who I am and take a moment to whisper my name to myself. If I can remember how to pronounce it.

I HAVEN'T SPOKEN to Woody Allen or Bob Dylan so everything in this chapter is mere speculation and in no way an attempt by me to imply a personal connection with either Woody or Bob other than imitating them in the shower.

When Woody and Bob were starting out there was one simple rule: if you can score more than 50 with your name in Scrabble, change it. So like thousands before them, Al Konigsberg and Rob Zimmerman went out and bought a pin and a copy of the Ohio phone directory.

It can't be easy, rejecting your name. The name your parents gave you, the name you grew up with, the name embroidered on your school socks. Psychologists describe it as a scarring and painful experience and that probably doesn't include the expenditure on new underwear.

Why did Al and Rob do it? As I say, I haven't spoken to them, and directory assistance have threatened legal action if I try again, so I can only speculate.

Did they believe that buried deep in our race-memory is a terror of being entertained by members of a different tribe? Unless, of course, Andrew Lloyd Webber wrote the music? Or did they simply fear the loss of their identities and thus fall prey to the age-old superstition that if a person's name isn't uttered, he or she doesn't exist, particularly in record shops?

I can't say for sure. But I sympathise with them because I too once changed my name.

I was young, I was naive and I desperately wanted to be an author. When I told my friends of my literary ambitions, they responded as one. 'You realise,' they both said, 'you won't be able to use the name Gleitzman.'

I was confused. Was another author already using it? I hunted through the library catalogue. The closest I could find was Morton Z. Gleftman, who'd written a history of solvents. Even if his readers spilt lots of the stuff on the cover of his book, it was unlikely to create confusion between us. I was planning to write racy post-modern thrillers with my name on the front in big embossed metallic letters that didn't include any post-graduate qualifications whatsoever.

My friends handed me a copy of *Halliwell's Filmgoer's Companion*. I stared at it. 'Halliwell looks nothing like Gleitzman,' I protested. 'Or is his first name Morris?'

They turned to the entry for Peter Lorre. Originally named, I read, Laszlo Loewenstein. Poor Laszlo, I thought. No wonder he always looked so doleful. A new name from central casting and he still had to spell it when booking a table at a truck-stop diner.

My friends pointed to the entry for Herbert Lom. Known to his parents as Herbert Kuchacevich ze Schluderpacheru. 'Morris Kuchacevich ze Schluderpacheru,' I said doubtfully. 'It's not bad, but it wouldn't leave much room on the front cover for a quote from a review. Specially one from the *Coonabarabran and Warrumbungle Examiner-Gazette*.'

My friends pursed their lips testily and tapped their fingers on the entry for Rita Hayworth, whose school socks had been embroidered Margarita Carmen Canino. 'I don't get it,' I said. 'Why would a studio make an actress sound so ordinary when they had under contract the only woman in the world named after a cocktail, an opera and a misprint?'

My friends sighed, closed the book and whacked me round the head with it. Suddenly I understood. 'Gleitzman's too much of a mouthful,' I said. 'If I want to be a bestselling author, I need something short, punchy, easy to remember. Something like Ed McBain or Patrick White.'

My friends nodded. I put my manuscript aside and set to work choosing a new name. I decided, after much deliberation, to hang onto some vestige of my identity by using an anagram of my real name.

Three years later, I finally hit on one, and thus my first stories were submitted under the punchy byline Lorin Zimmerstag. They were all rejected, as was the name when I discovered that in a certain Bavarian dialect it means 'room in a sanatorium where by day the bedpans are washed'.

Three weeks later, I received a summons from lawyers representing Lauren Zimmerstag, a writer of racy post-modern thrillers that were hugely successful in her native Austria. She was suing me. (And, it turned out, the compilers of a certain Bavarian dictionary.)

I didn't care. On the cover of the summons was my real name in big print. It looked good. I decided to stick with it.

InSENSiTiViTY

Mmm. Yes. I know.
Sybil Fawlty

In human relationships few qualities are valued as much as empathy. Some lucky people learn to be aware of and sensitive to the feelings of others very early in life. (They were probably the nipple-biters.) I'm still doing empathy evening classes, with the occasional full-day workshop.

WHEN I HEARD the kids talking about a big day out, I assumed they meant our normal big day out, i.e. a movie, a burger, a visit to the stationery store to see the really wide rolls of sticky tape, a browse through the humorous boxer shorts in a menswear shop and a happy but exhausting hour removing bags of peas from the super-market freezer cabinet using only our tongues.

So naturally I was intrigued when we got off the bus

at the Showground. 'Is there a frozen-food expo here?' I asked. 'Or a tongue surgeons' convention?'

The kids looked at each other and took a deep breath. 'Dad,' they said, 'this isn't that sort of big day out. It's the Big Day Out, a rock concert, 10 hours of deafening punk, grunge and heavy metal.'

'Oh good,' I said. 'I like music with a strong beat.'

'You'll hate it,' warned the kids. 'You'll be shocked, alienated, repulsed, appalled and outraged.'

'Don't be silly,' I laughed. 'I'm a modern parent. I'm hip. I'm funky. I wear *X-Files* pyjamas on the weekends.'

Inside, the music had started. The kids were right, it was loud, and I wasn't crazy about the way it made my internal organs vibrate. I put some liver sausage too close to the fridge motor once and it went all runny.

And the band didn't seem to be using very many notes. Just the one, in fact. I did think I heard a chord at one point, but it might just have been the next band in the dressing-room using a power saw to get a nose ring off.

The lyrics, however, were brilliant. The first number was about putting pets in the toilet, which spoke to me on a very deep level because I've been trying to buy a reasonably priced dog bath for months.

The group followed this up with a song about ducks. (I'm pretty sure that's what it was about. They'd cranked up the volume even more, which caused quite a bit of distortion and, I heard later, kidneys to vibrate on a restaurant table three kilometres away.) It was a very clever song anyway, even though I didn't under-stand all of it. What exactly is a duckwit?

'This is way cool,' I yelled to the kids. 'I'm having a fully groovy time. I think I'll go and have a mosh and a crowd surf and, if I can find someone with a strong enough nose ring, a hang-glide.'

That's when I noticed the kids were looking depressed and tearful. 'What's the matter?' I asked, concerned. 'Aren't you having a good time? Would you prefer me to take you to the electrical store to have another look at the fridge with the freezer at the bottom instead of the top?'

The kids looked at me sulkily. 'What we'd prefer,' they said, 'is for you to stop liking our music. How are we meant to challenge the dominant paradigm and redefine our place in society if you won't give us anything to rebel against?'

'But I have,' I protested heatedly. 'Chocolate milk's your favourite and mine's strawberry.'

'Leave our music alone,' shouted the kids. 'You've got your own. The Stones are still touring, at least in stadiums that don't have too many steps, and there's a rumour that Pink Floyd are going to record another album now they can get a pensioner discount on their electricity bill.'

I knew what the kids were saying, but I couldn't help it. The music that was rattling the old sheep droppings in the Showground was just too full of vibrant, intelligent, relevant ideas. As if to illustrate my point, a new band struck up with a wonderful song about fungal skin complaints. Once again it struck a chord deep inside me. I wanted to dive onto the stage and ask the lads if they'd been washing their dog in Dettol too.

Then I saw that my kids were leaving. 'Wait,' I called, 'don't go. There's another 28 bands to come.' As I raced after them I felt my scalp starting to burn in the sun 'Even though,' I said bitterly, 'I can understand you wanting to leave a hopeless venue like this. There must be 40,000 people here and shade for less than 4,000.'

The kids stopped and looked at each other. 'We like the venue,' they muttered sulkily. 'We like sunburn.'

I bought myself a drink to try to stave off dehydration in case one of the later bands played *Sailing* and I needed a cry. 'Two dollars forty for a tiny bottle of water,' I yelled indignantly to the kids. 'I'm appalled.'

The kids looked at each other again. I reeled away from the hot-food stand. 'Look at this so-called hamburger,' I shouted. 'The meat's overcooked, the bun isn't even sourdough and there's not a speck of yogurt and basil mayonnaise to be seen.'

The kids were grinning now. 'Yeah, well our generation likes being ripped off,' they said. 'Okay?'

Suddenly the heat and the noise and my vibrating spleen all started to get to me. I felt sick and dizzy. A small space became vacant on a shady bench in one of the old stands and I clawed my way through the crowd and flung myself down onto it. Within seconds I had a searing backache.

'Call this a wooden bench?' I screeched. 'A three-year-old could make a better wooden bench than this. It's an outrage.'

All around me faces were grinning mockingly. 'This wooden bench wasn't meant for your generation, Pops,' sneered a kid with green dreadlocks. On every side, young people started laughing and jeering. I turned to my kids for help. They were laughing and jeering too. One of them leant forward and put his lips to my ear. 'Thanks, Dad,' he whispered.

JEALOUSY

The jaundice of the soul.
John Dryden

*I try to be a bit more positive than that and use jealousy
as an emotional barometer. If I catch myself staying in
bed half the morning brooding and sulking about the
neighbours' house or car or breakfast cereal, I know I've
got unfulfilled emotional needs and I know only I can
fulfil them. That's usually when I move.*

I REALLY ENVY the white-breasted marsh-warbler. It has
this incredible sixth sense about where to build a safe and
quiet nest. Without needing a street directory or millions
of Sunday afternoons, it can pick a spot and know for sure
its new home won't be anywhere near a freeway or a naval
base or a white-breasted marsh-warbler shooters' club.

I'd give anything for that ability – money, my remaining

hair, even my collection of street directories and ordinance survey maps. If it would help I'd even pick lice off my body with my tongue.

But I fear I'm doomed to a lifetime of dud housing choices. Certainly the last two have been so dud I haven't been game to invite a single marsh-warbler home for fear of derision.

The first of the two was the house of my dreams. Elegantly proportioned, surrounded by space and trees, not a single hole in the guttering. It was situated on the far outskirts of the city where the air was clear and the days were tranquil. Or so I thought.

The day we moved in, the kids stopped and frowned. 'What's that rumbling noise in the distance?' they asked.

I cocked my head and preened my gardening jumper. 'It must be a waterfall,' I said. 'There must be a major river cascading off an escarpment nearby.'

The kids looked at each other and at the cheese rolls they were eating. 'What are all these black bits on our lunch?' they asked.

'Pollen,' I said and fell over. How those marsh-warblers scratch their heads with their feet I do not know.

That night the roaring and screeching started. I leapt out of bed to comfort the less worldly members of the family. 'Don't worry,' I said, 'it's quite normal. When you get this far from the city there are lion safari parks everywhere.'

There was another roar and another screech. 'Nature,' I said, 'in all its savage grandeur.'

The moppet whose head I was stroking looked at me wearily. 'Either that,' he said, 'or a Mack 16-wheeler hitting its air brakes on a freeway exit ramp.'

'What an imagination,' I chuckled.

The freeway exit ramp, we discovered the next day, was about 200 metres from the house, behind the trees. We soon realised it wasn't clarity sparkling in the air, it was bits of brake lining. Then the wind changed and the house filled with diesel fumes.

We stuck it out for a year. I shudder to think how much lead our bodies absorbed. Our dentist was wonderful, keeping us supplied with free surgical masks, but I noticed that whenever I was in the surgery he got me to stand between him and the X-ray machine.

One day I cracked. 'We're moving,' I said, 'to the inner city.'

The kids stared at me.

'What's the matter?' I asked. 'Have I got a big bit of brake lining on my nose?'

The kids shook their heads. 'No,' they said, 'but you've obviously got one between your ears.'

I protested that my study of urban demographics had revealed the inner city as the cleanest and quietest place to be. 'As the urban population grows,' I explained, 'industry and transport and freeways and lion parks move ever outward from the centre, leaving the inner city a tranquil oasis of leafy cafes and literary conversation.'

We moved to the inner city in the Christmas holidays. It certainly was tranquil. There wasn't a lot of literary conversation in our actual street, but I assumed that was because the neighbours were all indoors reading books. I was wrong. They were indoors pouring hot wax into their ears, desperately hoping it would set by the end of the holidays.

At six o'clock on the first morning after the holidays,

we were jolted from our sleep by a convoy of trucks thundering along our street. 'Maybe,' I croaked hopefully, 'it's the removalists with a few things we've forgotten.'

It wasn't. The trucks roared past our house, leaving our pyjamas coated with familiar black specks. 'Perhaps,' said a young voice, 'the navy's building a base further up the street.'

I rolled my eyes. 'What an imagination,' I sighed.

The naval base, we discovered later that morning, was being built just a bit further along the street than we'd ventured when inspecting the house. We went back to bed, depressed. Three minutes later the power-saws started. We got up and peered out the window and noticed for the first time how most of the adjoining houses had builders crawling over them. We went back to bed, sobbing.

Three minutes later the front doorbell rang. It was a neighbour. 'Great news,' he yelled excitedly. 'They're going to demolish the oil terminal.'

We stared at him blankly.

'The oil terminal down the street just past the naval base,' he said. 'It's a few hectares so it'll be a long and noisy job, but afterwards we'll have great water views. Well, I will because I'm going to build up.'

We've been going to bed early this year, to take advantage of the precious few hours of quiet before the trucks start thundering at six and the jackhammers start pounding at seven and the property developers start smacking their lips at seven-thirty.

Well, they were precious hours of quiet until recently, when a bird started using the tree outside our bedroom window to broadcast its mating call between three and six each morning. I don't know what type of bird it is, but after listening to its plaintive call for the past couple of months, I can say conclusively that it's not a white-breasted marsh-warbler.

LONELiNESS

No man is an island. Or a cay, or an atoll, or a bombora.

John Donne (paraphrased)

As a child I suffered intense separation anxiety.
If a parent or babysitter or pet had to leave the house
even briefly, I was thrown into a panic. I still don't know
if it was because I hadn't completed the developmental
stage known as individuation, or because we didn't
have a television.

WE WERE WATCHING a documentary on telly about Sardinian goatherds. 'Boy, I envy them,' I said. 'The clean mountain air. The independence. The really well-developed leg muscles.'

The kids rolled their eyes. 'Dad,' they said, 'Sardinian goatherds spend months each year in the hills without any human contact. Alone. Solo. Unaccompanied.'

'So?' I said.

'So,' they replied, 'it's not a great occupation for a bloke who panics when he's left in the house on his own.'

I knew they'd bring that up. Just because a person has one little anxiety attack and rings the police and the Samaritans and Meals on Wheels his family never lets him forget it.

'I thought,' I reminded them, 'you'd all gone on holiday and left me behind.'

The kids looked at me long-sufferingly. 'We told you several times,' they said, 'we were just going to the video store to return *Home Alone*.'

'I was having an off day,' I said. 'Normally I'm a mature, well-balanced adult who's completely at ease spending time without other people around.'

There was a pause while the kids struggled for oxygen. 'Name one substantial period of time,' they finally spluttered, 'you've spent alone. No friends. No acquaintances. No ringing up the talking clock for company.'

I reviewed my life. For some reason I seemed to have gone directly from living with Mum and Dad to living with fellow students to living with a girlfriend to living with a family. 'I went to an Ingmar Bergman Festival on my own in 1978,' I said. 'It was only 12 hours but it seemed longer.'

The kids weren't impressed.

'OK,' I said, 'I may not have spent much time on my own till now, but next month I'm going to drive across France to research a book. Seven days. Completely alone.'

A hush descended on the room. Even the Sardinian goatherds fell silent (though that may have been because they were biting the testicles off a young goat).

The kids shook their heads sadly. 'Thirty-six hours tops,' they said, 'and you'll be on the plane home.'

I was shocked. My own children, completely without faith in their father, just because I'd asked them to go with me once when I was having a session in a sensory deprivation tank.

'Not only will I survive seven days on my own in France,' I said, 'but I'll keep a diary to prove it.'

I did. Here it is:

Day One: Ah, bliss. Rolling along French country roads, my own master, responsible to nobody's agenda but my own. If I see an interesting little side road, I take it. If I come across a charming little lake, I swim in it. If it turns out to be on private property and an irate marquis aims his shotgun at me, I have only my own safety to consider and my own underwear to wrestle from his dog's mouth.

Day Two: Late start. It's more time-consuming than you'd think, picking shotgun pellets out of your bottom. Why are French hotel mirrors so high up on the wall? I was tempted to ask *le patron* for assistance, but I didn't want to shatter the fragile cathedral of my solitude. Plus his fingernails were filthy. Went to the *supermarché* to buy tweezers. Couldn't find any so had to make do with chopsticks.

The freedom of aloneness is endlessly exhilarating. I do what I want when I want. If I feel like tripe sausage and cooking-chocolate sandwiches for dinner I have them, unashamed and unintimidated by anyone else's views on the matter. Though the maître d' in the restaurant did give me a funny look when I ordered them.

Day Three: How hard it will be to rejoin human society and conform to the expectations of others. If another person had been with me in the car this afternoon, I bet they'd have kicked up an awful fuss about me driving on the wrong side of the road. If another person had been arrested with me, I bet they'd have panicked when I promised the arresting officer a bed for the duration of the Olympics and he waived the charges. I won't panic until he arrives in Australia and discovers I live in Melbourne.

Day Four: For the first time a couple of little signs that perhaps I might be experiencing a hint of loneliness. At one stage I caught myself talking to myself. (I don't know what about because my French isn't very good.) And at an autoroute service centre I was sure a drink machine winked at me. I didn't take it seriously, of course, and sure enough, after I'd been chatting to it for a couple of hours, I realised it was just the coin reject light flashing.

Day Five: In a small roadside cafe I cracked and asked the elderly *patronne* if I could live with her, her husband, their son and his de facto and their five children. I offered to sleep in the shed with the Renault. She threw me out.

Day Six: French provincial towns can be cold unfriendly places, specially if you go round knocking on doors pretending to be a Jehovah's Witness.

Day Seven: Spent the day driving high into the Alps in search of a community where friendship and camaraderie still exist. I found one, nestling under a mountain peak. Ah the relief of embracing a warm, living, if rather hairy, body. And goats don't smell nearly as bad as people claim in documentaries.

MANIPULATION

Just do it.
Nike

Just eat it.
Parent

Do you have a desperate desire to manipulate other people's lives for their own good and be swamped with their gratitude and admiration? If they won't let you, do you develop a powerful desire to kill them? Don't worry, there's a simple explanation. At some stage in your life you've spent time in a family. Or Canberra.

IT WAS THE broken election promises that started it. Not the Government's. Mine. 'Sorry, kids,' I said gravely, 'funding for the wide-screen TV with the six-speaker sound system and popcorn machine has been withdrawn.'

The kids stared at me, stunned. 'But you promised,' they said. 'You promised that if we elected to go without

Barrier Reef holidays and lollies and footwear, we could have a home entertainment system.'

'And so you can,' I said, handing them a yoyo and a harmonica. Before they could protest, I told them about the budgetary black hole I'd just discovered. 'It's going to take several billion dollars to plug,' I said.

For a sec I thought I'd done a federal treasurer and got away with it. Then the kids realised the black hole was in the guttering over our driveway. 'You can't just break a promise,' they wailed. 'We trusted you.'

I smiled patiently and sat the kids down and made one of the biggest mistakes of my life. 'Some promises,' I explained, 'are designed to be broken. Governments do it all the time. And if it's OK for governments to do it, it must be OK for parents, eh?'

The kids' eyes narrowed and a chill ran up my spine. I foolishly ignored it, thinking someone had just left the fridge door open.

The Canberra lobbyist arrived the next day, and before I knew it he was taking me to lunch.

While the waiter was pouring the champagne, the lobbyist handed me a package of glossy brochures and videos. 'Cast an eye over these,' he said, 'and I think you'll quickly see how much young people today can benefit from cutting school down to two days a week and eating lollies instead of meals.'

My eyes narrowed. I saw the contours of a piggy bank in the pocket of his Armani suit. 'Are you working for my kids?' I asked suspiciously.

'Sorry,' he replied smoothly, 'we never divulge the identity of our clients. Are you familiar with recent research statistics from Taiwan showing the very real contribution to child cognitive development made by wide-screen televisions?'

I stood up. 'Got to dash,' I said, 'there's a political crisis in the house.'

The lobbyist looked alarmed. 'Reps or Senate?' he asked.

'My place,' I replied.

On the way home I went to the library and frantically read books about the great political strategists of our time (Whitlam, Thatcher, Sylvester and Tweety Pie).

When the kids got back from school I was ready for them. 'The motion,' I announced, 'is that from now on, everyone in this family washes their own clothes and makes their own bed and scrapes their own plate and sets their own alarm clock and vacuums up their own dandruff. All those against?'

The kids raised their hands.

'All those in favour?'

I raised my hand. The kids looked smug. I looked at the goldfish, who raised their fins.

'Not fair,' cried the kids. 'This should be a conscience vote, not a factional numbers game.'

It was my turn to look smug. The goldfish looked pretty pleased with themselves too, since their elevation to the front bench. (It wasn't really the front bench, it was just a slightly higher shelf, but goldfish aren't that bright.)

'Family politics,' I pointed out to the kids, 'is a tough and ruthless business.'

Just how tough and ruthless I discovered the next morning. As I sat down at the breakfast table, I realised there wasn't a kid to be seen. Just a bunch of blokes in white overalls. 'G'day,' said one of them, 'we're the breakfast operatives.'

I didn't have a clue what he meant. 'Your kids,' he explained, 'have privatised themselves. From now on, their new company will be supplying all your offspring needs. You can choose your Basic Brekkie package, which is us sullenly chewing Coco Pops, but we recommend spending a bit more and taking the Parental Indulgence package which includes conversation and dish-rinsing.'

It was an expensive day. When the school operatives clocked on I forked out for the Deluxe Education package, which included paying attention in class and eating everything in their lunchbox. Then I realised too late that to get the men home safely I should have paid a Busy Road surcharge. The Deluxe included looking left and looking right, but not looking left again. By the time I'd paid for the ambulance and the laundering of the overalls, I was nearly skint.

I had only one option. At 4.30 p.m. I privatised too. I did consider only selling off 50 per cent of myself, but my underwriters were nervous that the market might not go for the bald patch without the paunch.

Dinner that night was chaos. I paid the required fee for Offspring Services Ltd to eat all their vegies, but the kids declined to pay Paternal Systems Inc to cook any.

Then we discovered that the Paternal Systems Platinum Platter package included ice-cream with the fruit salad, but due to a computer error the Offspring Services schedule of fees didn't include eating it as an available service. Things turned ugly. The PS technicians tried to force the ice-cream into the OS dinner operatives through their nostrils.

The kids and I looked at each other. We conceded that family politics was almost as silly as federal politics. Then we formed a bipartisan Nourishment Review Committee and went and had a pizza.

MARTYRDOM

You'll be the death of me.
Traditional family greeting

*Martyrdom used to be a noble quality involving sacrifice
and varicose veins. Lately, though, it's starting to be seen
as petty self-inflicted victimhood. If you've had the
unpleasant experience of being called a martyr by
someone who's not the Pope, here's a helpful hint.
You might not be dysfunctional after all. You might
just have been overseas.*

I'M JUST BACK from London and I'm still in shock.
Margaret Thatcher may have retired to the country to
bully roses, but there's still an underclass in Britain, a
fact I found pretty depressing. What I found even more
depressing is that it's us.

We Aussies would be better off if we weren't allowed

into the United Kingdom. I wish the authorities had just stamped my passport 'too poor' and escorted me straight back onto a plane to somewhere cheap like New Zealand. There'd have been much less humiliation that way. Specially for someone like me who'd been too busy getting ready for the trip to read the financial pages. (Don't suitcases take a lot of ironing?)

I should have sensed something was up when I joined the queue at the currency exchange booth at Heathrow and heard sniggering from people waiting to change Mexican pesos. Families with strollers full of roubles saw me and suddenly looked less self-conscious. I got a pitying stare from a bloke with two strings of beads and a cowrie shell.

But the full horror didn't hit me until I'd tossed my wad of Australian dollars onto the counter. 'Pounds sterling please, my good man,' I said to the clerk, 'and don't dally because I've got taxis to catch, pork pies to consume and large numbers of Roald Dahl books to buy, thus freeing up bookshop shelves for the works of lesser-known authors.'

The clerk counted my life savings, stuffed the whole lot into a Monopoly box and handed me a few notes. Four of them were banknotes and the other was the address of a soup kitchen. I chuckled good-naturedly. Obviously he'd confused the Australian dollar exchange rate with the pre-devaluation zloty exchange rate. He chuckled good-naturedly. No, he hadn't.

Fortunately there were other Aussies in the arrivals hall and I was able to locate them quickly by following the sounds of sobbing. We agreed that, given the woeful state of our national currency, we'd economise by sharing costs and hiding in each other's luggage on the tube.

I think I can say we experienced the full sweep of London's attractions, we just didn't experience them in much depth. Our ride in a black cab was fun as far as it went, which was to the end of the rank. Some of the others probably enjoyed our lunch at Simpsons On The Strand more than I did because, with 11 of us sharing one set meal, we could only have one food group each and I got the salt. The West End matinee was more exciting. I had a fantastic view and could hear every word sung. Admittedly it was over a bit quickly, but you rarely get more than two songs with buskers.

All in all, it was an enjoyable visit, even if it was for less than the 21 days I'd originally planned. When I got to the hotel and converted the tariff into dollars, I decided I'd have to cut my stay short. By 20 and a bit days.

Back on the plane home that night, I reflected on the lessons I'd learned. The most enjoyable parts of the visit for me weren't the expensive tourist traps, they were those fleeting experiences that are impossible to package or put a price on. The sun glinting on the Thames, the leaves falling in Regent's Park, the half a sandwich I found in the bin outside Harrod's. I think there's a lesson there for our casino builders and Olympics promoters. (More rubbish bins.)

A wise old travel agent once told me the secret of travel. It's a metaphor for life, he said, and if we focus only on the destination and forget to enjoy the journey, we'll be the poorer for it. Though he might have just said that because he was selling honeymoon packages to Mururoa Atoll.

If he was right, then I reckon exchange rates are metaphors too, possibly to do with our anxieties about being loved. If we were lucky we enjoyed parity exchange with our parents, but since then many of us live in irrational fear that the Swiss franc we've exchanged our freedom for may turn out to be a Malaysian ringgit.

I could be wrong, of course, but I'm afraid I'll have to leave you to sort it out because I'm flat out with my new travel project.

It's a guidebook for Aussie backpackers, those first casualties of an anaemic dollar. It'll show how to keep on top of costs in Britain using all the tricks, lurks and inside knowledge I picked up during my recent 24 hours there. I'm calling it *London On 900 Pork Belly Futures A Day*.

MASOCHISM

Warning: Smoking Kills
Advertising slogan

*Why are we so attracted to things that are bad for us?
The secret thrill of transgression? An 'up you' to
mortality? Cheap entertainment? Or is there another,
darker, reason why we can't stay away from booze,
fat, TV and parenthood?*

THE KIDS were aghast as they watched me unpack the
shopping. 'What's the matter?' I said. 'Don't you like
bread and milk?'

Then I realised what had happened. A bag had split
and they could see things that weren't for young eyes. At
first they could only point in horror. Then they regained
the power of speech. 'Skateboard safety accessories,' they
whispered, appalled.

Desperately I tried to hide the knee guards, elbow guards, wrist guards and crash helmet under a large tube of Dencorub. It was no good. 'We can't wear those,' wailed the kids. 'We'll be the laughing-stock of the whole street and the supermarket car park.'

Suddenly I knew I had to tell them the truth, no matter how painful it might be for them. 'They're for me,' I said, or tried to. Before I could get the words out I trod on a skateboard and flew across the kitchen, scraping my elbows on the floor, grazing my knees on the sink, jarring my wrists on the wall and banging my head on the fridge.

As my vision painfully cleared, I saw realisation dawning on the kids' faces. 'They're for you,' they said, relieved, running their fingers over the indentations in my forehead made by the fridge magnets.

Then they frowned. 'But you don't ride a skateboard,' they said. 'And you haven't touched rollerblades since you bought some and discovered they didn't give you a closer, smoother shave.'

It was time for a little talk. They were old enough to know the truth. As soon as I could stand up I sat them down.

'Remember when I told you about the facts of life?' I asked. They nodded, blushing. I blushed too. I'd hoped they'd forgotten how my working model of the human reproductive system had overheated and burnt a hole in the tablecloth. That was the last time I'd used Meccano for sex education.

I took a deep breath. 'I have a confession,' I said. 'There was one fact of life I didn't tell you about.'

The kids stared at me accusingly. 'So it's true what

they're whispering behind the tuckshop,' they said. 'When a woman's having a baby she does have to tip the anaesthetist.'

I sighed and went for a long walk. When I got back, I tripped over a bike in the driveway and fell into a science project in the front yard. I think it was a science project. It was a deep pool of mud half full of plastic dinosaurs. It might have been a political science project.

I sat the kids down again. They ran their fingers wonderingly over the indentations in my chin made by the plastic dinosaurs. 'Listen,' I said. 'You'll be having children of your own in a couple of decades, so this is something you should know in case you want to change your minds.' I took another deep breath. It was a brutal truth but I had to tell them. 'Having kids,' I said, 'is very dangerous.'

They rolled their eyes. 'We already know that,' they said. 'Mum told us about how dads drink eight Tia Marias before conception and try to take their trousers off over their heads.'

'I'm talking about after conception,' I said, blushing again. 'The 17 or 18 years after conception are very dangerous.'

The kids looked puzzled. 'We don't understand,' they said. 'Surely they're only dangerous if you leave your arms jammed down your trouser legs.'

There was only one thing for it. I took off my clothes. I stood before them wearing only my underpants and the Band-aid covering the serious paper cut I'd sustained from sitting on one of their body-piercing magazines.

I pointed to my feet. 'Chafed and misshapen,' I said,

'from queuing in amusement parks.' I pointed to my ankles. 'Teeth marks,' I said, 'from various of your pets.' I pointed to my knees. 'Tissue damage,' I said, 'from grovelling in front of teachers to further your education.' I pointed to my thighs. 'Stretch marks,' I said, 'from bending down to pick up after you.' I pointed to my tummy. 'Paunchy,' I said, 'from eating too much of your fast food.' I pointed to my grazed elbows, jarred wrists and dented head. 'I rest,' I said, 'my case.'

The kids looked at my battle-scarred parent's body for a long time. Then they sighed. I waited patiently for their tearful apology. Instead, they pointed to my feet.

'Chafed and misshapen,' they said, 'from throwing a tizz and kicking your rollerblades.' They pointed to my ankles. 'Teeth marks,' they said, 'from trying to use live rats for sex education purposes.' They pointed to my knees. 'Tissue damage,' they said, 'from grovelling under the bed looking for your Tia Maria bottle.' They pointed to my thighs. 'Stretch marks,' they said, 'from trying to stamp out a burning tablecloth while it was still on the table.' They pointed to my tummy. 'Paunchy,' they said, 'from eating too much of our fast food as well as your own.' They pointed to my elbows, wrists and head. 'Grazed, jarred and dented,' they said, 'from being a clumsy idiot.'

We looked at each other for a long time. Then I put my clothes back on. I winced as I bent down to do up my shoes, partly because of the plastic dinosaur in my underpants and partly because they'd reminded me that being a parent was even more dangerous than I'd believed.

They'd reminded me that not just our musculoskeletal

framework is at risk. Also at risk on a daily basis is an even more vulnerable body part. I put on my knee guards, elbow guards, wrist guards and crash helmet, but my ego still didn't feel safe.

MiSTAKES

Oooh, bugger.
Philosophy of life

*Educated in a binary right/wrong system, I entered adult
life convinced it was my human destiny to make
mistakes and be punished for them. Then I read in a
self-help book that mistakes aren't mistakes, they're
opportunities for growth. I've been much more relaxed
about making opportunities for growth ever since.
Except spelling ones.*

IT STARTED OUT as a touching gesture. I introduced the
kids to the new goldfish, brought out the muesli biscuits
I'd baked to celebrate the occasion, went into the kitchen
to make some tea, and when I returned they'd engraved
his name on his bowl. I was moved. 'What a thoughtful
and touching gesture,' I said. 'And generous too. Hiring

an engraving tool couldn't have been cheap.' The kids explained they'd done it without one, using a substance harder than glass. 'A diamond?' I said.

'No,' they said, 'one of your biscuits.'

I stared at the wobbly scratches on the bowl, so childish and innocent and only slightly clogged with charred crumbs, and I couldn't take offence. Not until I realised they'd misspelt his name.

'It's not W-A-Y-N-E,' I said. 'It's W-E-Y-N-E.'

The kids set about changing it, but I could tell they didn't approve. Little things gave them away. The tiny furrows in their brows, for example, and the way they shouted: 'This is bloody ridiculous.'

'I don't want him to have the same spelling as every other goldfish called Wayne,' I protested. 'I want him to be an individual, to stand out in the crowd.'

The kids took deep breaths. 'Dad,' they said quietly, 'what crowd? The only other things in the bowl are four litres of water and a bit of weed.'

I explained how unusual spellings of names produce unusual individuals. Barbra Streisand's and Siimon Reynolds' parents knew what they were doing. OK, even if they didn't, even if they were just bad spellers, look at the results. And imagine how much greater Barbra and Siimon's successes would have been if their family names had been Streiisand and Reynlds.

A few days later at a book fair my conviction was borne out. At first, anyway. A young reader glanced at the cover of my new book and screwed up her nose. 'Pretty dopey name for a book,' she said.

I shrugged, smiled and resisted the temptation to go and tamper with the brakes of her school bus. She pushed the book towards me. 'And what's your name?' I asked sweetly, signing pen poised.

'Kylee,' she said, 'with two "e"s.'

Silly me, I thought as I signed. Fancy mistaking her for a rude little madame when in fact she's a free-thinking and autonomous individual already well advanced along a unique and distinctive road through life thanks to the unique and distinctive spelling of her name.

'Bet you're glad your parents didn't opt for the conventional spelling,' I said as I handed her book back.

She glared at me. 'This is the conventional spelling,' she said. 'There are six of us in my class alone.'

The next young reader was Catherine. At least, I thought that was her name until I'd signed her book.

'No,' she wailed when she saw the inscription, 'it's not spelt like that.' I quickly changed it to Kathryn. 'No,' she sobbed. My next attempt was Katherine. Her sobs got louder. I tried Cathryn, then Catheryn, then Catharyn. She was bawling. People were looking. Book fair security guards were flicking through armed response manuals. I started to panic. What would people think I'd done? Told her my idea for a *Silence of the Lambs* pop-up book?

I racked my brains. Katharine. Kathyrine. Kathrin. Nothing silenced her sobs. Then, just as I was trying to force my pen into her tear-sodden fingers so she could sign the book herself, her friend arrived. 'It's K-A-T-H-E-R-Y-N-E,' said the friend.

Weak with relief, I amended the name and handed back the book. 'You'll thank your parents when you're older,' I said to Katheryne. 'When you're out there in the big wide world trying to get ahead in your chosen career, you'll be glad you're not just one of the crowd.'

Katheryne started sobbing again. Her friend took me to one side. 'She wants to be a movie extra,' she said.

The friend had a book for me to sign too. I took it and she told me her name. Determined not to make the same mistake again, I wrote in it 'G'day Gaele'. The friend smiled and shook her head. I tried Gaiyle. 'Nope,' she said. 'G-A-E-Y-L-E?' I ventured, wondering if I should give up inscribing readers' names in books and do their Medicare numbers instead.

'It's G-A-I-L,' said the friend.

I was shocked. I tried to think of something sympathetic to say. 'Must be tough,' I murmured.

'Not really,' said Gail. 'I was a bit self-conscious at first, then I realised that when I'm out there in the big wide world trying to get ahead in my chosen career I'll be glad I'm not just one of the crowd.' I stared at her. 'The crowd,' she said, 'of Gaeles, Gaiyles and Gaeyles.'

That afternoon I signed books for eight Kaits, six Brooces, seven Dayvids, four Charons, six Mykes, three Zoweys and five Rhons. And nine Weynes. Well, it would have been nine, but as the ninth was spelling his name I excused myself, rushed out of the book fair and jumped into a taxi.

'Faster,' I yelled at the driver as we wove through the traffic. 'A goldfish's sense of its own developing individuality is at stake.' By the time we'd screeched to a halt outside my place I'd chosen my pet's new name. A name that would set him well and truly apart from any crowds of goldfish he might encounter.

Kylie.

NARCISSISM

Moi.

Miss Piggy

Narcissists come in for a lot of hurtful criticism in self-help books, which I think is a bit unfair. I mean, what about megalomaniacs? They're much more of a nuisance than we are. They have to make other people fear them, whereas we're perfectly happy adoring ourselves.

IT WAS VERY EMBARRASSING. There I was, in the middle of a private act, one of those moments in life when you really want to be alone, and the kids walked in. 'Do you mind?' I asked indignantly. 'You know you're meant to knock.'

'But, Dad,' they protested, 'this is the kitchen.'

'Exactly,' I retorted. 'The one place in the house where a person should have a right to some privacy.'

I could see they weren't listening. Something had caught their eye. My breakfast. 'Dad,' they asked, 'why are you adding molasses, kelp and fish oil to your bacon sandwich?'

I sighed. They'd invaded my privacy this far, I might as well let them finish the job. 'I'm trying,' I said, with as much dignity as I could muster, 'to slow down the ageing process.'

The kids looked puzzled. 'But surely,' they said, 'if you want to stop a bacon sandwich getting old, you just put it in the fridge.'

Eventually, after much discussion, they grasped the concept. It wasn't easy for them, because it involved accepting (a) that someone over 35 would want to slow down his ageing process when he was so close to getting a pension, and (b) that someone over 35 could still chew bacon.

Once they'd twigged, though, they were extremely helpful. 'If you really want to delay the process of getting old and getting cheap teeth,' they said, 'you should try the new anti-ageing drugs that everyone's talking about.'

A tremor of excitement ran down my spine. Or it might just have been my inter-vertebral cell tissue deteriorating.

'Anti-ageing drugs?' I squeaked. 'Tell me more.'

'Dehydroepiandrosterone,' said the kids. 'Dimenthyl-aminoethanol. Melatonin. They're hormones that control the body's ageing processes. Oldies swear by them. Except the ones who try to smoke them.'

Eventually, after much discussion, I grasped the concept. By ingesting substances found naturally in the human body, substances used by the metabolism to prevent premature ageing, one could, according to some experts, slow down the ageing process even if one was already a bit old.

'Mind you,' said the kids, 'some experts reckon they can kill you faster. Specially if you try to carry too many home at once.'

I consulted a neuro-endocrinologist. I didn't want to be greedy so I asked his advice about only one of the new drugs. The one I could pronounce.

'Melatonin?' he said. 'Forget it. It's not available over the counter in this country.' I showed him the long piece of paper the kids had written the names of the other two drugs on. 'DHEA and DMAE aren't available either,' he said. 'You'll have to go to the US.'

'The US?' I said. 'And be exposed to the extreme ageing effect of international air travel? Skin structure collapse, cerebrospinal fluid dehydration, large-volume brain cell death, and that's just in the check-in queue.'

'Sorry,' said the neuro-endocrinologist. 'And now if you'll excuse me.'

I stared in disbelief. 'Is that all a highly trained specialist like you has got to say on the important subject of human ageing?' I said indignantly.

'Yes,' he said.

'Why?' I demanded.

'Because,' he said, wheeling his trolley round me, 'it's Saturday morning and this is the supermarket.'

I decided I'd have to take my mortality into my own hands. And so it was, a few days later, I found myself in a cavernous, darkened room lit only by mysterious blinking lights. Strange sounds filled the air. I swallowed nervously. I'd never been into an over-60s disco before.

I sidled up to a bloke taking a breather between

numbers and tapped on his walking frame. 'Hey, man,' I muttered, 'I want to score.'

With an obliging smile, he said: 'Two for 180.' I paused. That seemed a bit expensive, even for illegal drugs. Then I realised the old bloke hadn't finished speaking. 'Rain stopped play,' he said.

Eventually, after much discussion and the purchase by me of new batteries for his hearing aid, he grasped the concept. 'Get out of here before I call the police,' he shouted, 'you young delinquent.'

I scurried away through the dancing throng. White-haired couples paused mid-jive to glare at me. 'Dope fiend,' they hissed. The old bloke's voice pursued me to the door. 'We don't do drugs in here.' I think that's what he said. While he was speaking, a nurse clattered in noisily with a trolley full of small paper cups.

I went home and read everything I could find about circulating adrenal hormones and neurotransmitter boosters. I read how melatonin is produced by our pineal gland when our suprachiasmatic nuclei tell it to. I spent hours with a friend of mine, who's an actor, trying to disguise my voice to sound like suprachiasmatic nuclei. It didn't work.

I read how DHEA and DMAE are being given to mice in huge quantities in research laboratories. I wrote to a few of the labs, asking if, when they'd finished, I could have some of the mice, or even just a few cutlets. They didn't reply.

This story has a happy ending, though. Some friends of the kids were over the other day. I'd just finished pasting some new lipoic acid research data into my scrap-book. 'G'day,' I said cheerily to the new arrivals, and settled down to my embroidery. I'm doing the chemical symbol for melatonin on a placemat.

'Your dad looks well,' said one of the visitors.

'Yeah,' said one of the kids. 'It's his new hobby, it's taken years off him.'

NEEDINESS

Wilmaaaaaaa.
Fred Flintstone

The availability of self-help books means that these days we're tending to do our inner work in private, gripped by the fear that neediness is the bad breath of the new millennium. Which is a pity. I say bring back the good old days when folk gave each other a hand.

THE HOTEL MANAGER looked at me sternly. 'Is this true, sir?' he said. 'Did you ask this room service waitress to render you a service of an intimate nature?'

I couldn't meet his eyes. I felt sick with shame. I wanted to crawl inside my suitcase and wait for an airline to lose me. 'Yes,' I mumbled. 'It's true. I asked her to read me a bedtime story.'

'And it wasn't just me,' said the room service waitress,

trembling with indignation. 'He's tried it on with Gayle, Marge, Ron and the others.' She pointed around my room at the 11 trays. 'Plus he's had housekeeping up here four times.' She pointed to the ironing boards stacked against the wall. 'And George the concierge reckons the guest rang down claiming there was a very tiny spider in the bath and could George come up and bring his reading glasses.'

The manager looked at me with grim disapproval. 'Do you have anything else to say,' he growled, 'before I call the police and the Australian Library Association?'

Desperately, I tried to explain. 'Imagine you're far from home,' I said, 'doing a publicity tour for your new book. The only people you've spoken to all day are journalists who are cross because they can't spell your name, and publicists who are cross because you can't spell it either, and booksellers who are irate because you tried to shift your book to a better position and knocked over a pile of Bryce Courtenays. By the end of the day, wouldn't you crave that most sublime form of human intimacy, the bedtime story?'

The manager was unmoved. 'My name's Smith,' he said, 'and I know how to spell it.' His hand moved towards the phone. I knew my only hope was to make him understand, to let him hear the full and complete story of my lifelong craving to be read to. Luckily I had my diaries in my bag. I pulled out the first dozen or so volumes and started reading.

At a very early age, I came to love the sound of the human voice reading out loud. Mum was always reading things out – instruction leaflets on how to get baby sick out of carpets, directions for removing toddlers from vacuum cleaner bags, Proust's *A la Recherche du Temps Perdu* (in volume four there's a really good recipe for headlice drench).

Eventually I started to learn to read myself, and spent hundreds of hours under the bedclothes with a torch. I'll never forget the exciting day I was finally able to read the word Eveready.

But reading to myself wasn't the same, even though I did it out loud and put on other voices to try to trick myself. To be read to by another person, I realised one day as I sat in class drinking in the teacher's voice, was to have a lifeline flung across the chasm that separates us all. (A pretty significant achievement for a maths textbook.)

Years passed. I made my way out into the world. The loud, fast, busy, electric world where, I discovered, people rarely read to each other. I admit now I got a bit desperate. I must have sounded pretty silly on the phone each night begging the talking clock to say 'once upon a time'.

And getting myself arrested for shoplifting just so the police would read me my rights was very short-sighted. If I'd swindled shareholders and gone to Spain, they'd have had to read me an extradition order as well.

I shudder to think what might have happened if I hadn't finally met my dream partner, a woman who read to me in bed every night. She read from sex manuals, which was a bit exhausting, but at least we were both getting our needs met.

'If more people read to each other at bedtime,' I said to the hotel manager, my voice swelling with conviction, 'the widening chasm of cyberspace between us all would be bridged and the world would be a happier place, even if they weren't my books.'

I closed volume 19 of my diaries and waited for the manager to respond. He didn't. He was sprawled on the bed, fast asleep. The room service waitress was curled up next to her tray, snoring. I felt strangely fulfilled. Reading to other people, I realised, was as much fun as being read to. That didn't stop me ringing the porter. After he'd shifted the boss, perhaps he'd read me a quick chapter of Enid Blyton.

OBSESSIVENESS

If a thing's worth doing it's worth doing again in case you didn't turn the gas off the first time.

Ancient proverb

A word in defence of obsessions. They may be inconvenient, time-consuming and detrimental to our capacity for autonomous thought and action, but some of them, such as the one I'm about to share with you, contribute almost nothing to global warming. Thank you.

I WAS BROUGHT UP to believe that thrift is a virtue. In case I forgot, an embroidered panel hung on our kitchen wall. *Thrift*, it said, *Is A Virt*. Mum got it for a really good price at the school jumble sale after someone dropped a chainsaw.

They were thrifty times. Recycling hadn't been invented, but our place was a one-family energy exchange centre. String and rubber bands were carefully saved to be used again. Mostly to secure bundles of string and rubber bands as it turned out, but we didn't care because it felt virtuous.

Socks were darned, shoes were resoled, lights were turned off at night. (The big ones in the street were tricky. We had to use rocks.) If rice was thrown at a wedding, curry would be served at the reception. Newspapers were placed under carpets to minimise wear. (It worked brilliantly – I've still got some of those newspapers and they're hardly worn at all.)

Each sheet of Christmas wrapping paper was re-utilised until it had so much sticky tape on it we could use it as flypaper for the rest of the year. I didn't see brand-new wrapping paper until my 18th birthday. Ah, the first-time thrill of screwing it up and ripping it to shreds and throwing it in the garbage. Then I realised it was the present.

Times have changed. Recycling is a duty most of us observe, but where is that old-time passion for thrift? I don't see it in the eyes of maître ds in restaurants when I offer them my salad scraps for tomorrow's soup. Lift drivers are positively hostile when I suggest they use the stairs to save wear on the cables and rejoin me on the 18th floor. *Mortal Kombat*-playing youngsters don't even look up from their Nintendo screens when I drop hints about them grabbing a few chunks of flesh for pet food before moving on to the next level.

Thrift is no longer seen as a virt, I fear, and last week I realised why. I was in a bank queue and suddenly I noticed everybody was looking at me. At first, I was puzzled. I wasn't darning any socks. I wasn't rummaging through the wastebins looking for rubber bands or string. I wasn't getting distressed at the assistant manager's refusal to turn the burglar alarms off at night to save electricity.

I was just standing quietly waiting my turn and trying not to incur wear on my shoes. Then I realised what everyone was looking at – the coffee jar of five-cent pieces I was holding. I looked at everyone else in the queue. Nobody else was holding a coffee jar of five-cent pieces. They were holding deposit slips and wads of banknotes and gold credit cards and the title deeds to investment properties in the Bahamas, but no coffee jars. Not even sugar bowls.

I felt the shame of thrift colour my cheeks. I tried to look as though I was on my way to a coffee morning. 'Just withdrawing cash to buy Tim Tams,' I said to the people in front of me. 'The individually wrapped ones and to hell with the cost.'

I could see they didn't believe me, possibly because the overhead lights were making my coffee jar glint. (The money banks waste on electricity is criminal.)

I ignored the smirks and consoled myself. If that lot wanted to leave their five-cent pieces lying around in bedside drawers and down the backs of settees and inside pets instead of rolling up their sleeves and doing a bit of highly profitable work with a vacuum cleaner and a proctoscope, that was their business. We had another embroidered panel on the wall when I was a kid. It said, *Look After The Pennies And The Pounds Will Lo.* I've never known what it meant, but that morning in the bank I sensed it had some relevance.

Mercifully, a short 30 minutes later, I found myself in front of a teller. I handed him the jar. He explained that the coin-counting machine was the responsibility of the end teller. I rejoined the queue. The end teller was in the middle of going through a lengthy statement with a customer. They seemed to be trying to choose a supplementary Lotto number.

After another wait, during which my five-cent pieces took on only a slight patina of age, the end teller became free. When she saw my coffee jar, she rolled her eyes. 'This is going to take a while,' she said. 'These coin-counting machines aren't as fast as people think. And the electricity they use, it's criminal.'

I hung my head. The coin-counting machine hummed and tinkled. The teller handed me a button. 'Our dog eats them,' I explained. 'He thinks they're legal tender.'

Long minutes passed. I could feel the eyes of the people in the queue boring into me as they cursed my thrift. I didn't care. Soon all the hard work and stress and embarrassment would have paid off. The machine stopped. The teller handed me a $10 note and three more buttons.

I made sure all the people in the queue got a good look at the cash as I sauntered out. But they didn't seem very impressed. One of them, the manager of a sweat-shop, pressed his card into my hand and told me to give him a ring if I was interested in earning more than $5.70 an hour.

On the way home, I stopped at the fruit shop. Out the front was a huge crate of red capsicums for only $10. I had visions of delicious grilled capsicum. They wouldn't take long to do once I'd trimmed, cored, blanched and peeled them. I rushed inside. Next to the till was an embroidered panel. *Thrift*, it said, *Is A Virtual Impossibility*.

I spent the $10 on a cab home, to hell with the cost.

PANiC

Watch the trees.
My driving instructor

Wise words, and I try to bring them to mind when panic hits. Sadly, I haven't yet been able to. Scientists tell us the flight-or-fight response is one of our strongest drives, and panic must be what happens when we don't want to do either. The most I can remember at such times is to breathe deeply and wear lots of undies.

IF YOU ASKED ME 'What is the scariest experience you've ever had not involving spiders?' I'd reply, without hesitation, 'Going to a new school.' Just thinking about it brings all the anxiety, all the trepidation, all the gut-wrenching fear rushing back. I remember it as if it was yesterday. Which I suppose is understandable because it was yesterday.

A nine-year-old elbow summoned me from my restless sleep soon after dawn. 'Shake a leg, Dad,' said a cheery voice, 'we've got to be there in three hours.'

I forced my eyes open. It was my son, standing there proudly in his new uniform. The day I'd dreaded had finally arrived. I closed my eyes. 'I don't feel well enough to go to school today,' I moaned. 'I've got a tummy ache.'

'Come on, Dad, you'll feel better once you're up,' he said, dragging me to my feet. 'And it won't be so bad once you're there. Just a few forms to fill out and a bit of tuckshop duty to volunteer for.'

I clung desperately to the bedhead but he gently prised my fingers off with his new ruler. At the bedroom door I stopped and pretended I'd lost all feeling and movement in my lower body but he gave me a long-suffering look and showed me I hadn't with a newly sharpened pencil.

I locked myself in the bathroom and tried to loosen a filling so I'd have to go to the dentist instead, but the bubblegum I'd pinched from his lunchbox must have been defective.

'Dad,' he said softly after he'd come into the kitchen and caught me with my head in an oven bag trying to give myself a temperature. 'It's just an ordinary, everyday primary school. We'll be fine.'

I hated to shatter his naive confidence, but I couldn't help it. 'What if there are bullies?' I blurted out.

He sighed and gave me a reassuring hug. 'Dad,' he said. 'I'm tall for my age. It's very unlikely I'll be bullied.'

'I'm not talking about you.' I said tearfully, 'I'm talking about me. What if the principal gets me behind the bike shed and gives me a Chinese burn until I agree to coach the Year 4 baseball team? I don't know anything about baseball. I don't even know how you score a goal.'

My son, who'd been so understanding up till now, showed just a flicker of impatience. 'Dad,' he said. 'I'm the one enrolling.'

I paused in the middle of faking malaria. 'Yes,' I said, 'but I'm the one who's got to choose between nominating for the band committee and baking four dozen custard slices for the cake stall. You kids don't know what it's like for us parents starting a new school. The homework alone is crippling. You haven't even enrolled yet and I've had 87 pages of minutes from P&C meetings to read. What if they have a test?'

An hour later we stood at the school gate, both trembling, my son with excitement and me with fear and the after-effects of the 18 cups of black coffee I'd drunk to try to bring on a nosebleed.

'I just hope we got the uniform right,' I whispered.

'Relax,' said my son. 'T-shirt, shorts and long socks. It's spot on.'

I glanced anxiously around the playground. 'That's what you kept saying at home,' I muttered, 'but if all the other fathers turn up wearing suits I'm going to look a right dill with bare knees. I'll be ostracised by my peers and suffer serious developmental problems. They've done studies on it.'

My son took me by the hand and led me through the gate. We were met by a nice lady from the school office. 'You must be Year 6's visiting mime artist,' she said.

'No,' said my son, 'he's just pretending he's got St Vitus's dance.'

She nodded sympathetically. 'A lot of parents have first-day anxiety,' she said. 'The other day a new parent rang us wanting to know if he'd be beaten up if his chocolate crackles for the fete were soggy. Have you ever heard anything so ridiculous?'

My son looked at me. 'Yes,' he said.

I looked at the woman. 'Was that you I was speaking to?' I said.

My session with the school counsellor, though long, was entirely worthwhile. She took me on a guided tour of the school and helped me realise that many of my anxieties were groundless. My fear that I'd be ostracised because I wear glasses, for example, she disproved by introducing me to a group of other parents. Not one of them even commented on my specs. Most of them didn't take their eyes off my knees.

My anxiety about being given a really embarrassing nickname she dispelled by reminding me that nicknames are not given to hurt, rather to show fond acceptance.

'Thanks,' I said, relieved.

'That's okay, Fartypants,' she replied.

Finally, because she understood fear is so often based on ignorance, she patiently answered all my questions about school policy and procedures. And I must say I feel much more relaxed knowing what I should and shouldn't do. That I should include at least one of the basic food groups in my son's lunch, for example. And that I shouldn't drop him at school from a moving vehicle.

My son was waiting for me with the principal. 'Great news, Dad,' he said. 'You don't have to make custard slices or chocolate crackles if you come and talk to Year 4 about exotic diseases.'

I nodded happily.

'And teach St Vitus's dance to the baseball cheer squad,' said the principal.

So it actually worked out quite well, my first day, and now I'm feeling much better about school, which is just as well because I've got another nerve-racking ordeal coming up.

Cubs.

PARAnOiA

**Are you lookin' at me? Are you lookin' at me?
Are you lookin' at me?**
Taxi driver, en route to Sydney airport

I think we can all be permitted a little paranoia these days. In fact I'd go so far as to suggest that anyone who isn't a bit that way probably needs therapy. But we should try not to get carried away. Not everyone is trying to screw with our minds. Only hairdressers.

THIS IS A TRUE STORY and a disturbing one, so if you're feeling a bit fragile or you've had your hair dyed lately, don't read on.

I want to state right up front that I've never been one for conspiracy theories. I've always chosen to believe that JFK was actually killed by a stray bullet from a gun lobby rally in Fort Worth, and that John Kerr dismissed the Whitlam Government because the W page in his Rolodex was full.

So I was deeply shocked to discover in a suburban hairdresser's recently stark evidence of a conspiracy so far-reaching that the economic foundations of this country would be better off if they had termites and dry rot, plus serious subsidence because Noni and John left the hose running.

It all started when my partner went into the hairdresser's with a simple request. 'I'd like to slightly change the colour of my hair,' she said, 'so that when we find hairs in the bathroom sink at home we can tell whether they're mine or Old Baldy's.' (Or words to that effect. I wasn't actually there, but I've scientifically reconstructed the scene based on what she told me and the weight of probability.)

'I just want a colour rinse,' my partner said to the hairdresser, 'not a dye.' That part of the scene is verbatim, with the possible exception of the phrase 'not a dye'. My partner allows that she may have said, 'Not one of those effing dyes with the same chemical composition as Draino and rust-stripper.'

At any rate, the hairdresser, whose own hair could best be described as vivid, threw up her hands in disdain. (I'd better add 'allegedly' here in case this column is ever used as evidence by her other clients.)

'Darling,' she said (verbatim), 'look at all this grey' (reconstructed). My partner claims what the hairdresser actually said was, 'Look at these few tiny areas where your natural colour has faded ever so slightly, probably as a result of stress rather than age.

'A rinse won't cover this,' continued the hairdresser. 'You need a dye.'

My partner protested. The hairdresser rolled her eyes

and moaned to her colleagues about clients who won't leave it to the professionals. 'Darling,' she went on, 'you're too young not to dye.'

My partner is adamant this last quote is verbatim. She remembers wondering at the time if the hairdresser had just made it up or was quoting from a Jackie Collins novel.

'Besides,' concluded the hairdresser, 'hair dyes aren't made from harsh chemicals these days, trust me.'

My partner, anxious to accord the hairdresser all the status and dignity befitting a professional of many years' experience who had just referred to her as 'young', acquiesced.

An hour later she stormed into the house, face black. (With rage, not dye.) 'Look what that dumb bitch did,' she said (reconstructed). What she actually said was, 'I think the hairdresser may have misjudged,' but I knew what she meant.

Her hair was a slightly different colour, though the small streaks of stress de-pigmentation were still visible. Her hair was also a slightly different texture. She invited me to run my hand through it. I did and nearly lost a layer of skin.

'It's not as thick,' I said, trying to be positive. 'It'll be easier to brush, if you use a lubricant.'

My partner glowered. 'That's because,' she said, 'that dumb bitch (verbatim) has stripped most of the surface keratin off the hair shafts. The last time I saw strands this damaged they were flailing around the windscreen in an automatic car wash.'

I saw what she meant. I'm not saying her hair had a static electricity problem, but when she walked into the living room her head pointed towards the TV.

She went back and confronted the hairdresser. 'No problem, darling,' said the hairdresser. 'I've got some fabulous professional hair-care products here specially formulated for problem hair like yours.'

My partner considered assault, but decided her brittle shafts probably wouldn't have withstood the violent movement. Instead she bought $60 worth of shampoo and conditioner. The small print on the bottles said they were for 'chemically treated and severely damaged hair'. The big print said 'Guaranteed when purchased from a Professional Stylist only. Do not buy this product at any supermarket, drug store or other unauthorised retail outlet.'

Oh no, we cried at our place after we read that. Please let this just be a coincidence. Please let the hairdresser just be a dope and not a ruthless retail conspirator. Please don't let retail demand stimulation have stooped to such dastardly depths.

We tried not to think of other examples. The amount of tyre and suspension damage caused by misaligned manholes. The number of extra phone calls occasioned by people with Telstra Easycall forever having to say 'I'll call you back'. The widespread incidence of headaches caused by Muzak in chemist shops.

I fear the worst. The worry of it all is turning my hair grey. Look, there's one in the sink now.

PERFECTIONISM

You can't please everybody, not even 79.37826% of the time.
My high-school maths teacher

But that doesn't stop us trying, even though experts tell us the only approval that counts is from ourselves. For a while I concentrated all my efforts on earning praise from myself, but I found I was picky and impossible to please. So now I've gone back to trying to please everybody else, and all my appliances.

I'VE GOT A pretty rational mind except where chocolate and spiders are concerned. Plus I'm fairly well educated apart from maths and welding-equipment assembly. And I'm not currently on any medication that makes me dribble. Please remember these things when you read the next paragraph. I'll just run through them again. Very nearly rational. Very nearly educated. Absolutely no dribble. Okay. Here goes.

Daylight saving fades the curtains.

I know what you're probably thinking. Mushy-brained superstition, and his curtains must be made of chocolate.

Well, they're not. They're normal curtains and they've faded and it was daylight saving that did it. I've got several clear-thinking witnesses, including a cat.

It started when I tried to put our clocks forward last October. First on my list was the clock on the video. Naturally, as it's a digital clock, there was no little knob to turn. I checked, just in case, but there wasn't, so after a couple of hours I gave up looking for one. I reached for the instruction manual instead. Naturally, as it's an instruction manual, it wasn't there.

I found the instruction manual at 1.13 a.m. Why is it that instruction manuals never contain the most valuable instruction of all, i.e. 'Look for me behind the fridge'?

The manual listed 14 separate operations needed to change the time on the video. I performed them. The video indicated it was now set to record. I performed them again. The video advised it was no longer set to record. I extended the operations to 16 with the addition of pleading and threatening. The video replayed the episode of *Fawlty Towers* where Basil pleads with his car and then threatens it with a garden gnome. The car didn't budge either.

I gave up at 2.29 a.m. Eastern Standard Time and moved on to the oven clock. This was also digital, but at least it had knobs. In the interests of being absolutely thorough, and because I'm a perfectionist, I twiddled them all.

The clock didn't move. I decided to play it by the book. Not the instruction book, unfortunately, as eight months earlier that had been accidentally left in the oven while dinner was cooking. If only I'd noticed earlier in the meal that the lasagne was tougher than usual and had an index.

Without printed instructions, I had only one option. Keep twiddling. Our oven clock has four knobs and each twiddles in four different ways. By my calculation that meant I had 18,640 possible combinations of twiddle (estimate only). I finally got through them all at 4.56 a.m. (another estimate, as what the LCD clock panel on the oven actually said at this stage was 'Turn the beef').

I moved on to the clock on the phone. I was determined this one wouldn't beat me and so I persevered and persevered and didn't give up until the man in Helsinki I'd rung 11 times threatened to call Interpol.

Dawn was breaking (EST). So was my spirit. I made a list of all the other digital clocks in the house. Microwave. Answering machine. Hot-water timer. Fax. Personal organisers (two). Computers (four). Electronic pets (seven, we can't bear to break up the litter). Clock/radios. Radios. Clocks. I finished the list at 7 a.m. (9 p.m. Helsinki time). I realised that at the rate I was going I'd still be trying to put them forward on the day in March when I'd have to start putting them back.

Suddenly, slumped there by the phone next to the window, I felt overwhelmed. I buried my face in the curtains. And you can probably guess what my hot tears did to the cheap fabric. That's right, daylight saving doesn't only fade curtains, it shrinks them too.

PESSIMISM

Geneticists who claim that pessimism is an inherited trait are wrong. There is no pessimism gene. I challenge these so-called authorities to come up with one single example of new-born organisms that display pessimism. Except anchovies.

*My membership application
to the Royal Academy of Science
(abridged)*

I still maintain that pessimism is learned, probably in childhood shortly after you ask Dad if he's going to be OK getting your ball down from the roof without anyone holding the ladder or the compost bin it's balanced on and he says, 'Y—.' If you've been a pessimist from an early age, try to look on the bright side. At least you were prepared for adult life.

WANTED: SENIOR LOGISTICS ANALYST. Location: our place. Remuneration: an attractive package will be offered. I've already got the wrapping paper. If you're a logistics hotshot with more than 10 years' experience who's looking for the biggest challenge of your career, my problem-solving team needs you. I've got a situation here that's just too big for a poodle and a goldfish.

It all started with the side gate. Our home contents insurance requires that it be padlocked, which has been great for burglaries (none), but not so good for gas-meter readings (none).

The gas company have been very patient, partly because I've been doing most of the cooking over candles. But their patience and my non-stick frying pan have worn thin and they've issued an edict. Be home next Tuesday to let the meter person in. Offer him a cup of tea and a chocolate biscuit. (They didn't actually say that last bit, but I could tell from the tone of their letter that's what they meant.)

I asked the gas company if they could tell me what time the meter person would be coming. The gas company said they certainly could, and that it would be between 9 and 4.30. I thanked them politely. I know what can happen to people who are rude to gas companies. I saw *The Towering Inferno*.

Unfortunately, on Tuesday I've promised to be at a friend's place all day. His back doctor told him to get a new bed and he's having one delivered. The bed shop that stocks his orthopaedic model only delivers to his side of town on Tuesdays. My friend did consider transporting the bed home himself but his doctor advised against it as he hasn't got a car.

My friend asked the bed shop if they could tell him what time the bed would be coming. They said they certainly could, and that it would be between 8 and 4.30.

My friend thanked them politely. He knows what can happen to people who are rude to bed shops. He's read *The Princess and the Pea*.

Unfortunately my friend can't be at home on Tuesday because he moved into a new office last week and Tuesday is when the phone company is putting his phones in. They were meant to do it last Thursday but the technician booked for the job didn't turn up to work. Apparently he was having a bed delivered. (He lives on the other side of town.)

My friend asked the phone company if they could tell him what time the technician would be at his office on Tuesday. They said they couldn't be specific and that it would either be morning or afternoon and they'd ring him on Monday to let him know. He reminded them that they wouldn't be able to as there aren't any phones in his office.

Normally his business partner could be there all of Tuesday to wait for the phone company, but she's having plumbing problems. Her drains overflow every time the bloke next door empties his hot-water tank, which he's been doing every morning for the past week because he's been expecting an electrician to come and fix his heating element. The electrician keeps cancelling because he's just built himself a house and he's waiting for the power company to come and put the electricity on.

My friend's business partner booked a plumber last week, but he kept cancelling because he was waiting at home for a fridge mechanic who kept cancelling because he was waiting at home for a washing machine mechanic who kept cancelling because he was waiting at home to have something delivered. It couldn't have been a bed because it didn't arrive on Tuesday or Thursday.

It arrived on Friday morning, which meant the washing machine mechanic was able to do the fridge mechanic's washing machine on Friday afternoon and the fridge mechanic will be able to do the plumber's fridge on Monday but he can't say what time because he's got a freezer motor first thing and he might have to go across town for parts if the bearings are seized.

So the plumber can definitely do my friend's business partner's drains on Tuesday as long as his insurance company doesn't decide to send their assessor on that day. (The plumber was burgled. Thieves disguised as meter people kicked in his padlocked side gate.)

My problem, Senior Logistics Analyst, is that it's my birthday in five months. That's not very long to organise having the karaoke machine delivered for the party. Not when my brother-in-law's secretary's sister is thinking of having her carpets steam cleaned next week.

PhOBiAS

Men, you have nothing to fear except fear itself. And spiders.

General Patton
(not the famous one)

In my experience you can't cure a phobia overnight, not unless it involves non-matching bed linen. We have to find a way to live with our phobias. I find naming them can be a big help. For example, the phobia I'm about to reveal to you in this chapter I call Gavin.

UNACCUSTOMED AS I AM to sweeping statements, I would just like to say that surely the scariest experience for the occupants of this planet, with the possible exception of parrots and those waiters who recite more than 20 specials, is public speaking.

Well, it is for me. Only the other day I experienced the horror yet again. The dry mouth, the churning stomach, the throbbing red earlobes. I stood there, staring helplessly at the puzzled faces in front of me, wishing I was in Tibet under a bed. I could see the kids frantically gesturing for me to use my notes, but it was no good. My vocal cords had lost the power to produce words, even simple ones like 'a kilo of mince please'.

The butcher was very understanding. He sensed I wanted a kilo of something and gave me fillet steak. Walking home (we had to leave the car to pay for it), I reflected on the causes and origins of my tragic affliction (the public speaking, not the earlobes).

I know I wasn't born with it. I can clearly remember, at six months of age, uninhibitedly expressing myself in public. I can't remember now what about, but I suspect it would have concerned either the developing political crisis in Suez or the way strained apple and custard makes pureed brains curdle. I do know the bus was crowded and I communicated my feelings without any of the stress symptoms I experience as an adult except for a bit of light vomiting.

So what is it that destroys our innate capacity for relaxed public speaking? The education system? All those questions fired at us in class, none of them with easy answers? 'Smith, what's an isosceles triangle?' 'Potter, when was Shakespeare born?' 'Gleitzman, why have you got pencils stuck up your nostrils?'

Or is it the social furnace of puberty that strikes us dumb? I'll never forget the terror of crossing a crowded disco floor and going up to a group of young women and asking if any of them would like to dance or talk or fill out a joint application for a fixed-term housing loan. I found it hard to speak to any groups of people following that experience, even after the wire had been taken out of my jaw.

Psychologists tell us that fear of public speaking is actually a fear of public ridicule and humiliation. Could it be that this fear is a throwback to our tribal origins when every aspect of life was performed in the public gaze and every little mistake, mispronouncing 'epitome' for example, or cooking and serving a wild pig only to discover it was a relative, would result in ridicule from the tribe and a severe beating with large rocks?

Whatever the origins, it's a tragic and debilitating fear, and I decided a few years ago to confront and attempt to overcome it. I bought every public speaking manual I could find. There was one piece of advice they all gave (two pieces if you count remembering to face the audience). Speak in public, they all advised, at every opportunity.

That's exactly what I did. I gave a course of lectures on methods of wheat threshing in 17th-century Romania. I wasn't speaking to large numbers of people, in fact the train carriage often emptied while I was clearing my throat, but it was a start.

I stood for the school council and on the first Tuesday of each month I could be heard holding forth in the school hall on topics ranging from the role of compulsory education in a democracy to the correct way to wash basketball nets. Again, my audiences would have been larger if I'd actually been elected to the council and could have spoken at their meetings on the second Tuesday of each month, but the caretaker was a patient listener and it was good experience.

I gained more valuable experience speaking at my brother's wedding. I hadn't planned to, it was impetuous and spontaneous and I was surprised at how confidently my voice rang out across the assembled guests. In retrospect, though, I should have found something more appropriate to say than 'I do'.

Gradually my confidence grew, as did the delight of my publisher. Publishers like nothing better than authors who can talk about their books at conferences and literary lunches without fainting or drinking a bottle of vodka and trying to have sex with the audience.

I can, just, thanks to some advice I was given by an elderly Irish novelist of many years' experience. 'When my brains turn to mush,' he said, 'and I can't think of a coherent thing to say, I just read from one of my books.' Good advice, and I use it often, though my listeners are sometimes puzzled about why I'm reading from a book by an elderly Irish novelist.

We public speakers may seem relaxed and confident with our witty asides and bone-dry underwear, but behind the urbane facade always lurks the fear. I've checked with other authors, cabinet ministers, tour guides, press secretaries, lecturers, union officials, the people on the microphones in department stores, stand-up comics and archbishops. (Not all at once, in small groups.)

We all suffer the fear. We all wish we didn't. We're all sick of fillet steak. If there are any waiters or parrots reading this, help us, please.

REGRET

Doh.
Homer Simpson

The trick, I think, is to distinguish good regrets from bad regrets. Good regrets allow us to learn from our mistakes, complete our grieving, and make amends to those we have wronged. Bad regrets cause us to spend the rest of our lives boring people with details of the opportunities we've missed. Careful, don't get me started.

IT HAPPENED AGAIN TODAY. I was at the library looking for a book on fame and how to deal with the resulting stress symptoms, particularly the dry elbows. I'd just located a likely-looking volume and was rubbing some moisturiser into my arms prior to reaching up for it when I heard the horribly familiar sound of a child tugging at a parent's sleeve.

'Mum,' whispered a young voice, 'isn't that . . . ?'

I pressed myself against the shelves, desperately hoping to blend into the books around me. It was no good. Book spines don't come in Embarrassed Pink. I saw the mother staring at me and I knew that once again I and my elbows were about to pay the painful price of fame.

'You're right,' whispered the mother. 'It's him. The dopey bugger who knocked back the chance to write *Bananas in Pyjamas*.'

I ran. Normally I'd have stayed and tried to explain, but this morning I was already weak from an earlier encounter. At the hardware store, while I was paying for a paint scraper and some sandpaper, the whispering had started. I'd tried to ignore it, concentrating instead on explaining to the assistant that I was asking his advice about dry skin because my doctor was on holiday, and double-checking that number 5 was the best sandpaper for flaky elbows.

But the whispering was too loud to ignore. '*Bananas in Pyjamas*,' said the woman behind me. 'They offered him the job on a plate. TV scripts, books and videos, plus a percentage of the T-shirts, jigsaws, lunchboxes, toys, stationery and custard products.'

Her companion stared at me, eyes bulging with visions of royalties being delivered in very large plastic dump trucks. He himself was buying a *Bananas in Pyjamas* rivet gun.

'Get this,' scoffed the woman. 'The dopey bugger said no.'

Everyone in the queue gasped, then started to look sympathetic. My elbows started to itch. The sales assistant snatched the paint scraper back. 'Sorry,' he said, and explained that he wasn't allowed to sell sharp tools to the mentally deranged.

I just wish the sympathisers had been at my place that day a few years ago when I received the fateful call from the ABC. I bet if they'd had a producer from the children's television department asking *them* to write a series about tropical fruit in night attire, the words 'international merchandising phenomenon' wouldn't have leapt into their heads either.

I bet like me they'd have visualised a banana poking out of a pair of pyjamas, checked their diaries and the penalties for corrupting toddlers, and discovered that on that very day they were due to start a novel about glass-blowing in 14th-century Liechtenstein.

I tried to persuade the ABC to change the concept to something I could be more comfortable with. I explained that the man in my local fruit shop never put his bananas in pyjamas, all he did was toss a blanket over them and turn the light out. I pointed out that in the history of television there'd never been a successful series whose main characters turned black and squishy after five days in a bowl.

'Please,' I said, 'a writer needs to connect with his own truth. My work can only have integrity and passion if it flows from the wellspring of my experience.' It was no good. The ABC didn't think *Balding 37-Year-Old Caucasian Males in Pyjamas* had the same commercial ring to it.

I have no regrets. Well, not many. I do sometimes wish I hadn't gone around for two years after that phone call telling everyone I met that a series about two bananas who couldn't even dress themselves was doomed to oblivion. (I stopped when it finally dawned on me that everyone I was telling this to was wearing a T-shirt with two bananas on it.)

I do also wish that the two people who did accept the job and have been writing the series and the books and the videos ever since, pausing only to supervise the queue of cash-laden dump trucks backing up their driveways, wouldn't invite me quite so often to their holiday homes in Monaco and the Seychelles.

And of course I wish I could still have bananas in the house, but I'm sure you understand why I can't, particularly those of you who've experienced dry retching and hives.

My life isn't entirely taken up with regrets, though. Some days I feel real pride that I didn't sell out to the crass commercialism of the merchandisers. Though if anyone reading this is interested in marketing a range of miniature plastic 14th-century glass-blowers, my novel will be finished in a year or two.

And I've made some wonderful friends in the monthly No Regrets Support Group that I attend. There's the retired record company executive who declined to sign The Beatles, the Hollywood producer who thought *Pulp Fiction* was a hopeless script, and the merchandiser who had the opportunity to buy a 50-year licence to manufacture Teenage Mutant Ninja Turtle toys. He took it.

But my greatest solace has come from meeting a person who's suffered even more than I have. She's the graphic designer who created the physical appearance of the world's most famous bananas. I won't name her because I don't want her to have to suffer in the hardware store like me. I'll just tell you that because she was an ABC employee when she gave B1 and B2 the good looks that have helped them gross millions, she's not on holidays in the Seychelles this week either.

That's the way the banana splits.

RiGiDiTY

**The highest possible stage in moral culture
is when we recognise that we ought to
control our thoughts.**
Charles Darwin

*Trouble is, all we've got to control thoughts with are
thoughts. And before we know it, the controlling thoughts
have taken over. Martial law is declared between our ears.
Strict curfews are imposed on new ideas. We view all
change with deep suspicion. In a constantly changing
world, we become constant complainers. Oh well,
at least then we get to enjoy that sweetest of human
emotions, indignation.*

OUR POSTIE'S a really nice bloke. Good-humoured,
friendly and caring. I really appreciate the way he gives
me a sympathetic shrug when he delivers my gas bills.
He knows I find them distressing, mostly because I
haven't got the gas connected.

Everybody likes him. He can remember the name of everyone in our street, including their middle initial and tax file number, which in this harsh and impersonal world I find very touching.

But I'm worried about him. He's been very depressed lately. The other day I caught him having a quiet sob outside number 47. Even then he was his usual considerate self and didn't blow his nose on any of their magazines.

'What's the matter?' I asked, concerned. 'You haven't been bitten by a dog, have you?'

He shook his head.

'Licked a bit roughly by a dog?' I asked.

He shook his head again.

I persevered. 'By a kid?'

'No,' he sobbed, 'it's . . . it's . . .'

The poor man was so upset he couldn't speak. Sadly I watched him stumble away. Perhaps it's stress, I thought. It can't be easy, watching people's faces light up when you hand them an envelope from the gas company, and then seeing their disappointment when they find it's a bill and not a birthday card.

I decided to try to cheer him up. I wrote him a note telling him how much we all like him and got every resident in the street to sign it. Then I faxed it to him at the post office. The next day, when I saw him at my gate, I hurried out. His face was longer than a Postpak (one of the really long ones).

'Didn't you get my note?' I said.

He stopped what he was doing (there was no mail for me so he was giving my mailbox a dust and polish) and nodded sadly. 'I really appreciated it,' he said, 'particularly the fact that all the dogs signed it too.'

He took a deep breath, which didn't concern me at first because it was what he always did just before breathing on my street number and giving it a bit of a buff up. This time, though, he gave a long, ragged sigh. 'Why did you fax it,' he said, 'instead of posting it?'

I answered without thinking. 'Quicker and cheaper,' I said, 'and envelope glue brings my tongue out in a rash.'

The second I said it I felt like ordering a large boot from a mail-order company and kicking myself. But it was too late. His face was crumpling like a non-padded postbag. 'Nobody wants to post anything anymore,' he sobbed. 'They'd rather fax it or e-mail it or breathe it heavily into a phone.'

I stared at his bulging delivery bag. 'Looks like some people are still posting stuff,' I said encouragingly.

'Not for long,' replied the postie. 'Soon magazines will be downloaded from the Internet, bills will be processed entirely by computer, mail-order footwear will arrive by molecular displacement, and I'll be history.'

I called a residents' meeting in our street. 'We've got to start posting more stuff,' I said. 'Thank-you notes. Birthday cards. Thank-you notes for birthday cards. Don't just yell at the cat for being sick in the hydrangeas, send it a stiff letter.'

I could tell the other residents weren't keen on the idea. 'Your modes of discourse are seriously flawed,' said one. 'Information pathways are a shifting paradigm.'

I tried to argue the point, but the rash on my tongue made the long words too painful, so I gave up. I posted everyone six copies of the minutes, but it was no use.

'Sorry,' I wrote to the postie. 'I tried.'

The next day he was at my gate as usual, looking

almost cheery. 'If you'd like to help,' he said, 'fill in one of these.'

It was a glossy brochure titled *The Australian Family Lifestyle Survey* with a big Australia Post logo on it. 'Tell us what interests you and your family have,' it said, 'and we can make sure that you are kept fully up to date with new and exciting offers that you will be keen to hear about, completely FREE OF CHARGE.'

The brochure opened out into a 56-item questionnaire that wanted to know, among other things, my name, age, occupation, income, family statistics, leisure interests, magazine reading habits, supermarket allegiances, pet food consumption, car specifications, insurance renewal dates, phone usage patterns, credit card patronage, health insurance level, personal investment profile, takeaway food preferences and whether, when I'm in the doctor's waiting room, I watch the TV.

I stared at the postie, speechless.

'Isn't it great?' he grinned. 'Each one of these surveys, when completed, will cause thousands of pieces of direct-marketing mail to be dispatched. Via the post. You can have two if you like.'

He thrust a second one into my mailbox and saun-tered off down the street, whistling jauntily. I went inside, wrestling with a painful dilemma. I wanted to help him, I really did. I looked at the questionnaire. 'Does your family use or purchase any of the following?' it asked. 'Energy-saving bulbs, organic food, ready-made meals, compost heaps?' It was no good, I couldn't do it.

Instead I wrote to Australia Post, explaining that even in the name of friendship I wasn't prepared to expose the details of my compost heap for their commercial exploitation. I didn't put a stamp on the letter. I assume they, like commercial TV and radio, won't charge for their services once their primary purpose is to deliver advertising material. If they do, I'll complain. You may care to as well. Do it by mail. Every little bit helps.

SADNESS

Tragically I was an only twin.

Peter Cook

*Books on grieving tell us we spend most of our lives
doing it, some of us consciously, some of us through our
choice of kitchen tiles. We grieve for lost loved ones, lost
opportunities, lost ideals. Sometimes we tell ourselves that
everything's OK now, that we've finished being sad. But
then every four years there's another Olympics.*

IT WAS A simple matter, but an important one, so I waited
for everyone in the family to give me their full attention.

Two weeks later I was still waiting. Then the batteries
in the TV remote went flat on the same night that the
neighbours finally got curtains for their bathroom. It was
a God-given opportunity and I seized it.

'The Olympics,' I said, surveying the assembled kids,

pets, in-laws, partner and pot plants, 'are less than 806,000 minutes away, and it's about time this family started getting into the Olympic spirit.'

The family members looked at each other and frowned. 'What,' said a puzzled young voice, 'you mean ouzo?'

'I mean,' I said patiently, 'that even as I speak, tens of thousands of people around the world are working day and night to make these Olympics happen. Athletes tirelessly flushing their bodies of all steroids and artificial sweeteners. Starting-pistol manufacturers sending designers back to the drawing board to lose the silencers. Olympic officials locked in exhausting power struggles. The least we can do is show a bit of enthusiasm.'

The family members looked at each other again. For a long while there was silence, except for the whispered sound of someone explaining enthusiasm to a pot plant. Then a young voice spoke up.

'We'll think about it.'

I held my breath for two days. Not literally, of course, because if I could do that I'd be representing Australia in breath-holding at the Olympics.

Then, on the second evening, I was visited by a deputation consisting of two kids, a guinea pig and a rubber plant.

'We've given your proposal our fullest consideration,' said their spokesperson, 'and in our capacity as lessees of the lounge suite, we wish to announce that Olympic TV viewing tickets will be $395 for the armchair, $295 for the settee (shared facilities) and $145 for the beanbag, booking fee extra.'

'Lessees of the lounge suite?' I said. 'Since when?'

'Since we did a deal with the cats,' said the spokesperson, waving a signed and paw-printed contract under my nose. 'We get the lounge suite and they get the goldfish.'

Before I could protest at the ruthless barbarism of the deal, another deputation arrived. More kids and some mice. The kids were carrying plates of chocolate biscuits and the mice were tottering under chunks of exotic cheese.

'We're bidding for the right to have the second TV in our room for the duration of the Games,' said the kids. Before I could reply I found myself with an armful of Tim Tams and gorgonzola. One of the mice started doing a belly dance. Another gave me a topless calf-massage.

'Wait,' yelled the first deputation. 'The bidding process isn't over yet.'

And so I found myself swept away in a heady whirl of all-expenses-paid trips to the video arcade, all-expenses-paid trips to the 49 flavours ice-cream shop and, after fighting broke out over which bidding consortium would be inserting the 49th flavour into my mouth, an all-expenses-paid trip to the drycleaner.

I admit now my judgement was influenced. Looking back, I can accept that awarding second TV rights to a group consisting mostly of lizards and hydrangeas was a mistake. If the horse dressage events get boring they won't even be able to change channels.

But I was distracted by deeper concerns. These became impossible to ignore one day soon afterwards, as I was simultaneously negotiating to lower the Olympic parking fee in my own driveway to $40 a day and receiving bids from three groups who all wanted the exclusive right to charge the other groups for watching the old black and white set in the bathroom during aquatic events.

My heart sank as I watched young feet and assorted paws pounding the lino in a frenzy of artistic and cultural competition. Is this what it has come to, I thought wearily as another Tim Tam was shoved between my lips. (It might have been gorgonzola, I was beyond knowing.) Is this rabid commercial self-interest all that's left?

Then something wonderful happened. A young dancer slipped in a puddle of guinea-pig sweat and crashed to the floor. A young performer from an opposing consortium reached down and pulled her to her feet, even though in so doing he dropped several of the piggy banks he was juggling, thus compromising his consortium's bid.

My heart soared. Tears of relief pricked my eyes.

The Olympic spirit is not dead.

SELF-ABUSE

All sins are attempts to fill voids.
Simone Weil

Pain-relief, that's what it's all about apparently. When we fail to keep our hands above the sheets or out of the booze cupboard or away from Mars bar and apricot jam sandwiches, we're just trying to relieve the pain of our inner black holes. I like that concept, and I take solace from the knowledge that when I abuse myself, I do it out of genuine concern for my own wellbeing.

IT WAS ONE of the worst weeks of my life. On Monday, while I was watching *Friends*, the supermarket rang. Apparently there'd been a mix-up at the checkout and I'd taken the wrong bag. One of their customers had my lasagne and I had her panty pads. At least that explained why dinner was taking so long to cook.

Then on Wednesday, while I was telling the man in the fruit shop the good bits from the previous night's *Drew Carey Show*, I saw an old bloke shoplifting some onions. He looked pretty hungry, so instead of dobbing him in, I bought some onions myself and followed him. My plan was to swap my onions for his and return the stolen ones to the fruit shop. Unfortunately he went into another fruit shop and the people there thought I'd shoplifted the onions from them and hit me with a watermelon.

Finally on Friday, right in the middle of *Seinfeld*, the cat coughed up a fur ball with a Biro refill in it. No big deal, except that I'd thought the kids had taken my Biro refill so I'd made them buy me a new one and on the way home from the newsagent they'd accidentally dripped black ink on the neighbour's cat and had swapped our identical cat for it while they tried to clean it not knowing that earlier in the week I'd already swapped our cat for the neighbour's cat so I could take the neighbour's cat to the vet to have a half-cooked panty pad surgically removed from its stomach unaware that the kids would take the inky cat to the same vet for cleaning and that the vet would be depressed after discovering his father was stealing root vegetables and would mix the cats up and we wouldn't be able to work out which was which and the cats wouldn't tell us.

On Saturday morning I went to the doctor.

'I keep having these wacky, zany, crazy, mixed-up, laugh-a-minute experiences,' I said, 'and aspirin just aren't helping.'

I told her about my week.

'Could it be a male menopause thing,' I asked, 'or is it just a common medical condition like when Homer

Simpson got a bifurcate occlusion of the sacral membrane after trying to flatten a beer can between his buttocks?'

'Hmmm,' she said, peering into my eyes and ears. 'I'd say you have dangerously high levels.'

'What of?' I asked, panicking. 'Stress? Food additives? Lead? Onion soup?'

'Sitcoms,' she said. 'How many do you watch a week?'

'Not many,' I replied defensively. 'An average amount. Fifteen or sixteen. I'm not an addict, I only watch them with meals.'

'Perhaps,' the doctor said gently, 'you should try cutting back.'

'Circumcision?' I said. 'How would that help?'

She looked at me for a long time. We both knew she was right.

The TV had to go. I went home, dragged it out to the car, drove to a high cliff and hurled it over the edge. Unfortunately it fell on a family picnicking below. My son captured the whole thing on tape and we won the grand prize on *Australia's Funniest Home Videos*. Six TVs.

I'm not proud of what I did next. Normally I'm a mild-mannered, easygoing person who wouldn't dream of trying to destroy an entertainment genre from the inside, but I was desperate.

I started writing sitcom scripts. I wrote one for *The Nanny* in which Fran becomes a nun and goes to live in a convent and takes a vow of silence and keeps it.

I wrote an episode of *Friends* where the entire cast sit down and watch an old episode of *Married with Children* and get so depressed at what life has in store for them that they kill themselves.

I wrote a *Seinfeld* script that was truly about nothing. I don't know if my 42 blank pages ever reached Jerry, but if they did, it would have been around the time he announced he was ending the show.

I do feel a bit guilty about that. When he was in Australia, I went to his hotel to apologise. 'Jerry,' I planned to say, 'I'm sorry about your series, but I was trying to stop sitcoms taking over the world.' And I would have said it too, if I hadn't got trapped in a lift with a transsexual aerobics instructor and a paraplegic fundamentalist on their honeymoon.

(Memo to TV producers: All spin-off rights to this chapter are still available.)

SELF-DECEPTION

Love is never having to say you're sorry.
Traditional Hollywood greeting

Why shouldn't we kid ourselves a little? Why shouldn't we treat ourselves to a few fondly held fallacies about ourselves? Why shouldn't we take the occasional break from our fearless pursuit of inner truth and wallow in the illusion that our bathrooms are clean?

I DIDN'T TAKE the news well. None of us at our place did. We felt deeply hurt and very indignant, and I know I'm speaking for all 87,000,000,000,000,000,000,000,000,000,000 of us.

The news was delivered by the son of some friends. 'You do realise,' he said two seconds after walking in, 'that this house is filthy?' I was so taken aback I nearly dropped the vacuum cleaner nozzle I was polishing.

I'm not saying I'm houseproud, but I do like to keep the place clean. Floors swept, walls wiped, toaster vacuumed. Plus I'm a stickler for not letting dust build up in a bathroom, particularly down the back of the hairbrush sterilising unit. And I insist on regularly shampooing the carpets, even though it is an effort getting them into the shower each morning.

I waited for the boy's parents to tell him off and make him apologise for his rudeness. And ground him for a year and make him clean the toilet with a toothbrush. (A new one, of course. How people expect to get a toilet clean with a dirty toothbrush is beyond me.) Then I remembered his parents were still outside putting on the surgical overboots I ask my guests to wear.

'Bacteria,' said the boy cheerfully. 'The whole place is crawling with them.'

I was more than certain it couldn't be, but you can't be too careful so I grabbed the flyswat. (I don't like spraying the house with dirty chemicals.)

'That flyswat, for example,' said the boy. 'Covered in bacteria.'

I peered at the woven plastic, warm and squeaky-clean from the dishwasher.

'There's about a billion on that,' said the boy airily.

'How do you know?' I retorted. 'Got a microscope in your pocket, have you?'

As it turned out, he had. A big one. Fifteen seconds later I was seeing a very different flyswat. A craggy, pitted surface covered with millions of sausage-shaped bacteria, some of them waving tiny flies away from their faces.

The vacuum cleaner nozzle was worse. What looked

like gleaming chrome to the naked eye was actually a boulder-strewn slope covered with mono-cellular organisms clinging on desperately by their fingernails, their hair pointing towards the mouth of the nozzle.

I felt faint. I fanned myself with the flyswat, then wished I hadn't. I followed the helpful boy and his microscope around my once-pristine house. Soon I was feeling even fainter.

An almost new kitchen sponge, used once and boiled twice, was revealed to be a Telstra-sized tangle of thick cables swarming with plump little bacteria with jam round their mouths.

The toaster, once I'd removed it from its dustcover, metamorphosed under the lens into a moonscape of scorched food particles and deeply tanned grain weevils relaxing on beach towels.

Down the back of the hairbrush sterilising unit in the bathroom was what I at first took to be a secret detergent storage dump, probably created by me in case I ever had to wash a bathplug in a hurry.

'Flakes of skin,' said the boy.

I looked closer. He was right. The coloured specks weren't optical brighteners, they were dust mites in picnic attire.

After many more such horrors, we finally arrived at my pride and joy, the lounge suite. 'Don't bother,' I said. 'You won't find anything here. This lounge suite has been steam-cleaned, vacuumed, brushed, dusted, sponged, aired, beaten and, as you can see, covered in thick plastic. Plus I use a deodorant under its arms.'

The boy stuck a microscope slide down the back of a cushion. Soon I was staring into a scene from *Jurassic*

Park before they vacuumed the dinosaurs. Fearsome creatures lumbered through a primeval landscape of hair, food particles and bits of dead insect, muttering to each other to get out of the way so they could see the telly. I slumped back, a broken man.

The boy's parents consoled me. 'We felt exactly the same,' they said, 'right after we bought Dougie the microscope for Christmas. We boiled that plum pudding for eight hours, but if you listened carefully you could still hear it joining in the carols.'

'There's only one thing to do,' I sobbed.

The boy stopped poking around between my toes and looked up. 'Get a stronger microscope,' he suggested, 'so we can see the micro-organisms on the micro-organisms?'

I shook my head. 'Start living,' I said, 'in plastic bubbles.'

My friends smiled. Or perhaps it was just the single-cell organisms on their skin tugging playfully at the corners of their mouths.

'There is another option,' they said. 'Learn to live with them.'

That's what I've been trying to do for the past few weeks. It's going quite well, actually. I like the feeling of never being alone in the house, specially late at night, and I'm looking forward to having some help with the cleaning, just as soon as I can find some really small floor mops.

Sure, we have our disagreements. I've had to chide those bacteria a few times about making the milk in the fridge go off without replacing it, and those pesky amoebae are always putting my glasses where I can't find them.

But I guess I think of them all as family now. I realised this the other day when I was visiting a friend in the country. A neighbour was over, bragging about the extent of his property. 'I've got 35,000 head of livestock on my place,' he said.

'Is that all?' I said. 'I've got 87,000,000,000,000,000, 000,000,000,000,000,000 on mine.'

ShAmE

They've axed my show. Shame, Channel Seven, shame.

Derryn Hinch

Few of us, say the self-help books, come out of childhood without a bit of shame buried deep beneath the lolly wrappers and puppy fat. To have true happiness as adults, they tell us, we should liberate ourselves from shame. Trouble is, I've seen people without shame and they always make me want to change channels.

I'VE JUST SEEN a wildlife documentary and I'm ashamed. I realise now how narrow-minded I've been about molluscs. I've only ever thought about shellfish in terms of price per kilo and whether they'd scare the cat. I've never stopped to think how like us they are, if you leave aside blood temperature and driving ability.

Did you know, for example, that oysters can

communicate with each other? In really sophisticated ways too, not just tapping on each other's shells with small rocks. And whelks have fantastically complex social structures with vertically integrated hierarchies and lots of aunties. And marine biologists have discovered that when baby clams are separated from their parents, the parents actually express grief and sadness as well as the usual warnings about staying away from garlic butter.

By the end of the program, I was sobbing too. That final fish market sequence was heartbreaking. Thousands of molluscs just lying there, lonely, scared and worried about missing next week's PTA meeting.

After the end credits, I pulled myself together, went to the kitchen, gathered up every last oyster and mussel and clam, drove them to the beach, apologised to them and placed them gently back into the water. It was a futile gesture. The tins just sank.

As I stood watching the labels bobbing on the surface and the seagulls screeching overhead looking for a can-opener, I made a promise to myself never to eat shellfish again. How can I, now I know how much we've got in common? They've even got the same taste in television as us. (They didn't watch *Echo Point* either.)

It's a big decision and you probably think I won't stick to it, but I will. I stuck to my decision not to eat lamb or beef, and that wildlife documentary about sheep and cattle was ages ago now. (I know, strictly speaking, sheep and cattle aren't wildlife, but they got pretty wild in the documentary when the truck turned off at the abattoir instead of going on to Surfers.)

I'll never forget what that documentary taught me: that

dumb animals feel emotion just as much as we do, plus, in the case of sheep, they're better at remembering birthdays. Suddenly, I knew that steak and chops were off my menu for good. I could no more eat those sensitive, feeling creatures than I could my own brother-in-law, even though he hasn't remembered my birthday in years.

But I didn't have to forgo red meat entirely because that same week kangaroo came on the market. Enthusiastically I braised it, roasted it, barbecued it and served it with custard. (I'm not a very good cook.) Then ABC-TV screened one of the best wildlife documentaries about kangaroos ever made and I was mortified. How could I have not realised how incredibly like us kangaroos are, if you leave aside shoe size and the fact that the plastic shopping bag is unknown to them?

As I sat watching that magnificent great grey kangaroo letting his kids stay up too late in an attempt to win back their affection, I felt a bond so powerful I simply couldn't finish eating one of his relatives.

I picked up the plate, drove to the Pilbara and gave the leftovers a decent burial. Or would have done if a bush rat hadn't eaten them while I was digging the hole. Instead, I shed a few tears and uttered a few words to mark the solemn occasion. 'Bugger it,' I said quietly. 'There goes another source of protein.'

That's the trouble with wildlife documentaries these days. They're too good. We learn far more about a species than ever before, and usually at dinner time. Thanks to modern lightweight equipment, wildlife telly is full of camera lenses poking into places we've only ever seen garlic poked into. Little wonder we end up bonding with our burger.

It can be fascinating and moving, but it does make planning a week's menus very difficult. Every time I pass the chicken shop and see feet on special, I resist the temptation to buy up big in case that week's Olivia Newton-John documentary reveals that chooks are, in fact, deeply sensitive creatures with a superb sense of rhythm and that they did the backing vocals on her last single.

The people in the fish shop have lost all patience with me just because I insisted on a signed note from the fisherman certifying that the fish had died from natural causes. When I said it should include details of any last will and testament specifying cooking method, they banned me. They reckoned I was being too fussy for someone who was only buying fish fingers.

So I'd like to send a plea to the producers of wildlife documentaries. You've shown us the cute, lovable, sensitive, fascinating, well-brought-up side of the earth's creatures. Now can we please, please, please have some films showing us what little shits they can be?

There must be molluscs who mistreat their kids and stab their workmates in the back or the underneath or wherever molluscs stab each other.

And I can't believe that out of more than a billion sheep in the world, there aren't at least half a dozen who throw litter out of moving vehicles and play loud music late at night.

If you could get your cameras out to them as quickly as possible, I for one would be very grateful because I think I'm developing a protein deficiency. And if en route you stumble across any likeable, intelligent, engaging tofu, please put the lens cap back on.

STRESS

Put your head between your thighs.
St John's Ambulance first aid manual
(banned edition)

*OK, stress is the number one killer today, but let's look
on the positive side. Stress has given us art, scientific
discovery, religion and technology. Mosses and
lichen don't experience stress, and where's their
electronics industry?*

WHEN WE MOVED in and discovered one lot of our
neighbours were nuns, we were delighted. You may not
know this, but statistics show that nuns have very few
parties involving commercial disco equipment, they
rarely abuse pets physically and their frequency rate of
tuning motorbikes after midnight is way below the
national average.

We looked happily ahead to years of blissful peace

and quiet, broken only occasionally by the soft pop of communion wine corks and the gentle murmur of excited voices during ecclesiastical questions on *Sale of the Century*.

'Hooray,' I said very quietly, anxious not to disturb the serenity of the immediate neighbourhood. 'Yippee,' I whispered. I didn't go so far as saying 'Thank God', an omission I now fear may have caused much of the horror that followed.

I can't remember how soon afterwards it was that I realised how wrong I'd been about the joys of domestic nun proximity. As my audio-cognitive therapist said the other day, 'A person can't be exposed to the sort of noise levels you've been exposed to, Mr G, and still expect to have a fully functioning short-term memory and penis.' At least, I think that's what he said. My lip-reading's still not great.

I may be vague about the timing, but not about the other awful details. Shortly after breakfast one morning, our place started to vibrate with the roar of a powerful engine. Naturally we assumed it was just a semi dropping off a container-load of souvenirs for a forthcoming papal visit.

An hour later the house was still shuddering. And the roar of the engine had been joined by the even louder noise of water smashing into brickwork with massive force. I went and knocked on the nuns' front door, fearful lest a miracle may have gone astray and Niagara Falls, instead of materialising in the Sudanese desert, may have been erroneously relocated to a suburban patio near our place.

The nuns weren't home and I soon saw why. In their

driveway was a very large compressor roaring away without the benefit of any sound insulation whatsoever. I was puzzled. I knew nuns sometimes took a vow of silence, but I couldn't remember hearing of any who'd taken a vow to make as much noise as possible.

A thick hose ran from the compressor into the nuns' backyard, where, when I peeped over the back fence, I saw a figure in a sort of space-suit blasting mould off the brickwork with thousands of litres of water a second. Three or four hours later, when I finally managed to attract the figure's attention and the figure turned off the hose, I reminded the figure that mould could be removed from brickwork with a little light brushing. I humbly invoked the memory of Mother Teresa and her habit of gentle traditional labour, and her other habit of never renting 2,000-horsepower compressors.

The figure removed his helmet, revealing himself to be not a nun but a surly subcontractor of no recognisable denomination. In the biblical spirit of his employers, however, he did tell me to go forth and multiply.

The rest of that day was deafening, but since then blissful silence has reigned. OK, there has been a slight buzzing, but you expect that with inner-ear trauma.

Until this morning. Shortly after breakfast our place began to vibrate with the roar of powerful chainsaws. I hurried outside, thinking the nuns might need a hand pruning their roses. Instead I saw that the magnificent tree in their backyard, a towering prince of trees that has gladdened the hearts of neighbouring households for decades, was being ripped down by a team of men in overalls. Possibly monks who'd taken a vow of wood-chipping, I didn't enquire.

Instead I asked the foreman why this was happening. 'Termites,' he yelled. He didn't say how many, but from his hand movements I could tell it was dozens. I couldn't hear much of what he was saying, but I gathered that the tree's fate had been recently decided by the nuns, and possibly the Vatican.

As I sit here, the chainsaws roaring on, the mechanical wood-mulcher out in the street sounding like the very jaws of hell, I can't help but reflect. If I'd given up my life to the service of the God of my understanding, when it came to brick mould or termites I think I'd pray for a bit of divine intervention before I brought in the boys with their noisy toys.

Perhaps I'm being uncharitable. Or just unrealistic. One thing seems likely though. No longer are charity, grace, pity, kindness and truth the only prerequisites for entry into heaven. I fear we may also need earplugs.

STUBBORNNESS

A powerful idea communicates some of its power to the man who contradicts it.

Marcel Proust

I can't find a single self-help book that gives advice on how to become less stubborn. That must mean it's OK to be pig-headed and ornery. So if you've been gritting your teeth trying to be less stubborn, relax. Though now I've suggested it you probably won't want to.

THE TRAVEL AGENT was being a bit stubborn. 'No,' he said, 'and if you ask again I'll lose my temper.'

I looked at him pleadingly. 'Go on,' I said, 'just this once.'

The travel agent's lips went thin. 'I warned you,' he said and entered a code into his computer which meant that the next time I stayed in a hotel or motel I'd be sent to bed early without any dinner.

'It's not fair,' I said. 'Everyone else is going on adventure holidays and hang-gliding and abseiling and white water rafting and scuba diving and bonding with crocodiles. Why can't I?'

'Because,' said the travel agent, 'you threw up on the paddle steamer in the Echuca museum, you got vertigo inspecting a tall lupin at the Toowoomba Carnival of Flowers, and when you reached up to the top shelf just now for that *Explore Tasmania by Rope* brochure you had a nosebleed. Now stop being silly and go home.'

I brooded for a while. Then I let him have it.

'All right,' I shouted (I had to shout because I was halfway home and I was worried he wouldn't hear me), 'if I can't have an adventure holiday, I'll have an adventure life.'

I started immediately, crossing the road at a Don't Walk sign. It probably wasn't as heady as bungee jumping off the Big Pineapple or hurtling down the Franklin in a rubber inflatable without satellite navigation equipment, but it was pretty exciting, and there was lots of flying spray from the mouths of passing truckies. By the time I'd dried my oilskins and caught my breath, I knew a life of danger and excitement was for me.

I hurried home and tore up my house insurance policy, my car insurance policy, my life insurance policy, my income insurance policy and a policy I'd only recently taken out which insured all my policy documents against termite attack and being taken on an adventure holiday by a careless insurance broker.

It was a spine-tingling moment as the last scrap of Plain English fluttered to the floor. I didn't stand there savouring it for long, though. There was too much adrenaline flowing through my veins and too many staples sticking into my feet. Instead I busied myself going round the house removing the deadlocks from all the doors, windows and cat flaps. What a sense of liberation as the last flap swung free. I could see that the cat, who'd been sitting outside for the past two years trying to work out how to use a key, felt it too.

Next I disconnected the burglar alarm, the exterior security lighting and the video surveillance system. I almost chickened out and left the video surveillance system connected because it has been so fantastic. It's a camera trained on the front door with a monitor inside so you can see exactly which videos the kids are bringing into the house.

But there's no chickening out when you're in pursuit of excitement and danger, so out it went. Followed by the safety circuit breakers on the power board. These stop a power surge melting your vacuum cleaner if a short circuit occurs, as it often does when you accidentally vacuum up your coffee. I almost chickened out with this one too, but then I asked myself, do they have circuit breakers on hang-gliders? No they don't. Click.

Then it was into the bathroom and kitchen, throwing out excitement-suppressants at every turn. Do they have non-slip shower mats on hang-gliders? Bath handrails? Oven gloves? Carving knife storage blocks? Microwave door release delay circuits? (Actually I think they might have oven gloves. Either that or the cold air makes their fingers swell.)

Boy, I thought as I filled another garbage bag, no wonder people go on adventure holidays. Most suburban dwellers are so insulated from risk and danger, about the only thing they don't have is cotton balls in their wall cavities.

I was halfway through removing the cotton balls from my wall cavities when the doorbell rang. In the old days I would have answered with the words recommended by my insurance company: 'You are an uninvited person on my premises. I cannot provide you with a drink of water as my plumbing is defective. I cannot let you use my telephone as it is out of order. If you do not leave my premises immediately I will turn the hose on you and ring the police.'

Instead I just sang out, 'It's open, come in, don't trip over the melted vacuum cleaner.' The travel agent came in, followed by a party of weather-beaten folk in anoraks and climbing boots. They saw my shower mat in the garbage and their faces lit up.

'Gee,' they said to the travel agent, 'when you told us the Franklin was drought-affected and the bungee rope had gone bung and the hang-gliders were in having new oven gloves fitted we thought our adventure holiday was stuffed but this is fantastic.'

They ran off to encounter the cat flaps and the drawers full of unsheathed knives. 'You haven't got any brochures, have you?' asked the travel agent sheepishly.

I had brochures printed the next day and now I'm booked out till the end of the year. It's exhausting work running adventure holidays, and fairly hard on the living room carpet, but I love it. The best part's coming up with new adventure ideas. Next month I'm taking them to the Carnival of Flowers.

STUPiDiTY

Against stupidity the gods themselves struggle in vain.
Friedrich von Schiller

*I struggle in vain against it too, but I try not to let it get
me down. True, a lot of my stupid behaviour is distressing
to witness, particularly when it involves greed, fear or
mishandled power tools. But at other times, so I'm told,
my stupidity can be quite touching.*

I'VE NEVER HAD much success with wild animals. A
possum moved into my roof cavity once, but my clumsy
attempts at nurturing only drove it away. I forgot how
sensitive wild creatures are to sudden noises. I should
never have used power tools on the Cape Cod extension
I built for it.

I formed quite a good relationship with a cockroach
briefly, but I think it felt I was smothering it. When I

suggested it have my bedroom and I move in behind the fridge, it went next door.

Apart from that, my encounters with wild creatures have been riddled with mutual misunderstanding, suspicion and fear of picking up an infection from dirty incisors. I tried to kiss a koala once and it ran off in a panic to get tetanus shots.

So when I saw a bear the other week, a large and untamed grizzly ambling along a mountain road in Canada, I should have wound up my window, stuffed my travel insurance certificate into the glove box and driven on.

I'm not sure why I didn't. A desire to connect with something elemental in an increasingly manufactured world probably, and the fact that I'm very stupid.

At first things went well. I pulled up alongside the bear and smiled winningly through the open window. The bear looked at me with interest. I thought I saw the hint of a smile, though the movement of the lips might have been caused by some small animal struggling to get out from between its incisors.

I pointed to my neck to show I didn't have a camera around it and therefore wouldn't be attempting to diminish the bear's personal dignity with happy snaps. The bear blinked, in gratitude it seemed to me, though it's possible a wolverine it had just eaten was giving it wind.

As I gazed at that magnificent creature, wild and primitive and free, something primitive stirred inside me and I had a powerful desire to tear off my clothes, run into the woods, daub my body with ancient tribal markings and spend the night at a camp site that didn't have a TV room in the amenities block.

I quelled the desire. And the urge to take the bear home with me so the whole family could experience its wild grandeur and be put in touch with their primitive selves and stop using so much expensive hair conditioner. I knew I'd never get anything that furry through Customs, not even if I forged it a passport in the name of Hinch.

Oh well, I thought, at least I'm lucky enough to be having this life-affirming experience. I reached through the window to pat the bear and start bonding.

The bear stood up. It was my turn to blink. I hadn't realised it had been slouching. As its shadow fell across the car, I wondered if I should mention the health problems bad posture can cause in later life. Then I saw its claws and wondered if I should mention the health problems shredded skin can cause almost immediately.

Our eyes met. The bear's looked a bit bloodshot and I hoped it wasn't feeling grumpy after being up late eating raccoons. It took a few steps towards the car. I decided I'd better introduce myself in case it thought I was a big-game hunter or an industrial chemist with some cosmetics to test.

'G'day,' I said. 'I'm an Australian children's author over here to publicise my books, none of which are about teddies losing their stuffing or getting dropped in the bath or registering blood alcohol levels of more than 0.05 per cent, honest.'

The bear growled and moved closer. I could smell the faint odour of raccoon terrine. The worrying thought hit me that this creature probably weighed more than all my luggage put together. If it pulled me out of the car and sat on me, I'd be crushed. Even more seriously than when my luggage fell off the overhead rack on the airport bus. And there were its teeth. They were even bigger and sharper and more brutally carnivorous than the bus driver's.

It was a difficult moment. Would I wind the window up and introduce an impenetrable barrier between two creatures yearning to connect on a primal level? Or would I leave the window down and hope the other creature wasn't yearning to connect on a jugular level?

How often through the ages must man and beast have faced this dilemma. How different the history of our planet might have been if more humans had kept their finger off the driver's side automatic window button.

I decided to do my bit to foster a new era of understanding between two species who had until now viewed each other primarily as lunch and rug.

'I love your country,' I said. 'Specially the timber-derived furnishing products.'

The bear growled angrily. For a second I thought it must have had a relative in the plastics industry. Then I realised it was glaring at the car seat covers. The black, furry car seat covers with the brown chocolate stains.

'They're nylon,' I explained. 'Actually a polymetri-acetate compound I think.' For a moment, the forest fell silent. Then the bear lunged.

I hit the button. As the window whirred up and I floored the accelerator, I felt strangely elated. We'd been together for nearly a minute, that bear and me. It was a start.

I drove on, keeping my eyes peeled for cockroaches.

SULKING

**I'm not sulking, I'd just rather have
my dinner in this cupboard.**

*Australian author after failing to
win literary prize*

*I haven't really got any advice to offer about sulking
except don't do what I did and forget to take cutlery
into the cupboard. Oh, and try to be understanding
when you encounter sulking in others.*

BOY, WAS I WRONG. I assumed it would be the kids
who'd be feeling neglected and resentful after my recent
overseas trip, but it wasn't, it was the appliances.

The kids barely knew I'd been away. When I arrived
from the airport and flung my arms around them and
hugged them tearfully, they looked confused.

'Jeez, I missed you in Canada,' I said.

They stared at me. 'Canada?' they said. 'We thought
you were down at the newsagent's with your hand

trapped under a pile of body-building magazines again.'

I forgave them when I saw they were whipping something up in the blender. It had to be a welcome-home cake.

'What a lovely thought,' I said, tasting the mixture. The kids looked exasperated. 'Don't eat it all,' they said. 'Our pet lizard will die if you eat its puréed grasshoppers.'

Just then the blender stopped. 'Now you've broken it,' sighed the kids. 'It was working perfectly earlier this morning, before you re-entered the country.'

I stopped retching. 'Earlier when you were making my welcome-home cake?' I asked hopefully.

The kids shook their heads. 'Earlier when we were running our homework through the blender so it would look like it had been chewed up by savage dogs.'

I pressed the start button a few times. The motor didn't move, just growled faintly. At the time, I assumed that was the noise blenders made when they'd got a half-finished history project in their juice extraction duct. It wasn't until much later that I realised it was the sound of an appliance sulking.

The kids went out to get their lizard a pizza and I sat down at the computer. I like to get my thankyou letters done as soon as possible after a trip. Hospitality deserves a speedy response, as does bringing a massive aircraft safely down onto a narrow strip of tarmac without hitting my place.

I switched the computer on. All was well until I'd typed the first few words ('Dear Flight Crew, Thank you from everyone on board QF12, and in particular everyone in my street ...'). Then suddenly the screen filled with bizarre computer hieroglyphics. I was stunned. I'd never seen anything like it before. I hadn't even realised my computer was made in Egypt.

I tried everything I could think of. Nothing worked, not hitting the Escape key or the SetUp key or the Ctrl Alt keys or my head on the screen.

Even then I didn't get the message. I stared at those symbols for ages and only afterwards did I realise how many of them looked like little frowning computer monitors. And how many others looked like little pouting printers. I don't know what a sulky silicon chip looks like, but there were probably a few of those too.

The truth didn't hit me until I finally gave up on the computer, chiding myself for not spending the extra on a Please Give Me One More Chance And I'll Never Do It Again key, and sat down to watch my *Splendour Of The Rockies* video.

The first disappointment came when I looked closely at the packaging and saw it was covered with mountains and didn't have a single shot of Sylvester Stallone in boxing gloves.

I sighed and put the video in the VCR anyway. It wouldn't go in. I tried a different cassette. That wouldn't go in either. The loading mechanism seemed to be jammed. The machine wouldn't even accept its very favourite video of all, the heart-warming tale of a kidnapped puppy who's saved by a video machine.

I switched on the TV news to catch up with what had been happening while I was away. The screen stayed dark. 'Come on,' I said to the TV, 'some stuff must have happened. Or was it all at night?' The screen stayed dark.

I couldn't believe it. I'd only been back 15 minutes and four appliances weren't working.

I called a repair company. The serviceman took one look at the blender, the computer, the video and the TV and turned to me grimly.

'On your recent trip,' he said, 'did you think to send any of these appliances a postcard?' Actually he didn't say that exactly, what he said was, 'I'll have to take them back to the workshop', but I knew what he meant. I hung my head and told him I'd forgotten.

'And I don't suppose you thought to bring them anything back?' he said. 'Key rings? Tea-towels? A snowstorm in a Perspex bubble, preferably falling on a small Canadian appliance?' He didn't use those actual words. The ones he used were, 'The parts could take a few weeks,' but I knew what he was really saying.

'I've got some placemats,' I said. 'Grandeur Of The Rockies.' The serviceman gave me a strange look. I knew what that look was saying. 'If they haven't got Sylvester Stallone on them, don't bother.'

I don't know what the serviceman did at that workshop, but within a couple of weeks the blender, the computer and the TV were all home and working perfectly. I reckon he did more than just change a few capacitors. From the size of the bill, I reckon a psychotherapist was involved.

The video, though, is still sulking. I've lost count of how many times it's been back to the workshop. Each time it works fine for the serviceman, but the minute I get it home it refuses to play. I've apologised, I've pleaded, I've flung my arms around it and hugged it tearfully, all to no avail.

I reckon the video's doing it on purpose, to make a point. If I have to keep driving the video to the workshop for much longer, soon it'll have covered the same distance as a return trip to Canada.

SUPERSTITION

Superstition is the religion of feeble minds.
Edmund Burke

Self-help gurus in the eighteenth century weren't as respectful of their clients' feelings as most are today. Confide a superstition to a therapist today and you'll probably be invited to honour it, own it and understand it. Understanding a superstition is essential before you can let go of it, but unfortunately that can take years. I'm just hoping I live long enough.

THE FIRST TIME I nearly died was 30 years ago and, looking back now, I'm certain the Queen didn't mean to do it.

Well, fairly certain. It seems unlikely a reigning monarch would summon the captain of the royal yacht *Britannia* as it motored up Sydney Harbour and instruct him to direct the vessel's wash at my modest craft's distant mooring in an attempt to drown me, but she might have done. Particularly if she thought I was a fox.

Whether she did or not, my four-and-a-half-foot, single-masted dinghy was no match for the royal tidal wave that socked it in the gunnel. It capsized, taking me with it, weighed down as I was by a large-print edition of *Moby-Dick*.

Under the water I carried out all the survival manoeuvres I'd seen on *The Poseidon Adventure*: holding my breath, thrashing about wildly, screaming for Shelley Winters. Nothing worked.

Then I realised I was tangled up in the wires from the mast. My brain secreted a chemical whose name I've forgotten, the searing pain in my chest stopped, I accepted calmly I was about to die and allowed my lungs to fill with water and royal diesel effluent.

Fortunately some very kind people whose names I've also forgotten (I don't think Her Majesty was among them) dived in and righted the dinghy, catapulting me into the sunlight where I lay for some time, embracing life and coughing up plankton.

That was in May 1970. In May 1972 I nearly died again. A Mini-Moke giving me a lift was hit by an overtaking car on the Federal Highway just outside Canberra. The Moke became airborne and flipped over. For one-and-a-half seconds things didn't look too good for me and the other three occupants. Mokes don't have solid roofs or roll bars and we didn't have big cushions strapped to our heads.

But we didn't die, thanks to a tree. The tree stopped the Moke hitting the bitumen upside down. Instead it hit the tree at a 45-degree angle. We lay in a heap against our saviour's trunk, bruised, concussed and extremely grateful it was still a tree and not a box of tissues in a funeral director's office in Osaka.

Later, after I'd regained the power to think chronologically, I noted briefly that my two near-death experiences had both happened in May. But I didn't have time to dwell on it, caught up as I was in my new mission: to persuade the people of Australia to plant a million trees, most of them along the Federal Highway just outside Canberra.

I didn't think about the coincidence for another eight years, until May 1980, when I nearly died again. I switched on the desk lamp in a motel unit in Essendon and found myself hurtling backwards across the room. For a moment I thought I was merely reacting to the puce and mauve and green lampshade, but after I'd hit the wall and sunk to the carpet I saw the small black hole in my thumb and smelt charred flesh and realised I'd just had enough volts through me to power warning lights on the *Britannia*.

It turned out the previous guest had taken the desk lamp switch cover as well as the towels and the ashtray, leaving the metal terminal exposed. It was a chilling discovery, but not so chilling as the discovery that it was May. That discovery unnerved me so much I forgot to sue anybody or check to see if my pee glowed in the dark.

Once I'd regained the power of speech I gave myself a stern talking to. This is no time to get superstitious, I told myself. Bad things happen in threes, I told myself, including May near-death experiences. You've had three, I told myself (once I'd regained the ability to hold up my fingers), so stop worrying and get on with your life.

Which I did, right up until May 1987, when I nearly died again. My car was hit by a negligently driven four-wheel drive on a suburban street. You're probably thinking I was out of my mind going anywhere near negligently driven four-wheel drives in May. I had the same thought myself at the moment of impact. All I can say is there's nothing like sharing a driving seat with a crankcase to focus the mind on what month of the year it is.

Since then, Mays have been mercifully accident-free for me, mostly because there aren't that many accidents that can happen under my bed, not since I reinforced the legs and put extra padding on the fluff.

I've spent the time wondering, why May? Could it be just coincidence? Or fate? Or karma? In a past life could I really have been that unkind to a reigning monarch about his or her desk lamp?

Or does astrology hold the answer? Is the time of our demise written in the stars, but in my case only the month is visible because the year is obscured by an empty space shuttle pizza box?

Or is the explanation purely pragmatic? Perhaps I'm just more accident-prone in May. Perhaps that's when my blood-sugar level has finally dropped after Christmas lunch.

Whatever the answer, dear readers, as my difficult time of the year approaches, I ask for your assistance. I'll have to come out from under the bed at some stage and venture down to the shops for more crash helmets and shin-pads. If you could strap a couple of mattresses to your recreational vehicles and 80,000-tonne yachts I'd be hugely grateful for ever and (hopefully) ever.

TiDiNESS

Eureka!
Archimedes' cleaner, on finding the bathplug under the kitchen sink behind a pile of old socks.

These are tough times for those of us whose modest needs include indexed filing systems for our dirty washing and lettuce that can be ironed. We're condemned as control freaks, poor frightened souls who couldn't go with the flow if we fell off Niagara Falls. Will the world ever acknowledge the contribution tidiness has made to its health and happiness? Probably not.

IT WAS A TASK that required all the concentration I could muster. I took several deep breaths to get extra oxygen to my brain and other major organs. Then I felt a young hand tugging at my sleeve. 'Dad,' said a young voice, 'we want to talk to you about something.'

I sighed. 'Please, not now,' I said. 'I'm trying to tidy my wardrobe.'

'It can't wait,' said another young voice.

I sighed again. Then I reminded myself that a child's desire to communicate is a precious thing. With a rush of emotion I remembered the very first words my son had ever uttered. ('Dad, you've just sat on some green bubblegum.') I turned to the kids, misty-eyed. Forgive me.' I said. 'What is it you want to talk about?'

'You being a mass murderer,' said the 12-year-old, 'and an arsonist.'

I wasn't sure I'd heard her right at first, distracted as I was by the can of spray-on chocolate ice-cream topping she was pointing at me.

'And a kidnapper and an enemy of the State,' said the nine-year-old, taking aim with a can of fizzy blackcurrant juice.

'Don't be silly,' I said. 'When have I ever killed large numbers of people?'

The kids looked at me levelly. 'You haven't,' they said. 'Yet.'

For a moment I panicked. Could there be some horrible family secret the doctors were keeping from me? A defective gene? A really bad temper? A tendency to violent psychosis triggered by using dandruff shampoo more than twice a week?

'Do you remember,' said the kids, 'what you said to us last weekend when you made us tidy our wardrobes?'

I forced my mind back. 'Um . . . something about what a shame they don't make bulldozers small enough to fit through bedroom doors?'

The kids shook their heads. I thought harder.

'Something about remembering to hold hankies over your noses while fumigating?'

The kids shook their heads again. 'You said, and we quote, "You can tell a lot about people from their wardrobes."'

They held up a copy of *True Crimes* magazine. 'Recognise this?' they asked. It was a photo of a wardrobe. It could have belonged to anyone, me or a million other people who keep all their black shirts together and all their white shirts together and all their blue shirts together and who don't own shirts of more than one colour because you never know which section to hang them in.

'The owner of this wardrobe,' said the kids, 'killed 18 people with a snowplough, six of them in their own lounge rooms.'

I looked at the page more closely and could see immediately it was the wardrobe of a psychopath. Three of the white shirts weren't on white hangers.

The kids turned the page. 'Recognise this?' they said.

I shrugged. It was an ordinary-looking wardrobe with the shoes lined up, as one would expect, in descending order of heel wear.

'The owner of this wardrobe,' said the kids, 'burnt down 87 ice-cream parlours in a three-year period. His plea of insanity was accepted.'

I studied the photo. 'I'm not surprised,' I replied. 'Some of those pairs of shoes have got the right shoe on the left and the left shoe on the right.'

The kids sighed and turned the page again. 'You must recognise this,' they said.

I have to admit that for a moment my heart stopped. The pile of jeans on the shelf, stacked in ascending order of fabric fade, did look eerily familiar.

'The owner of this wardrobe,' said the kids gravely, 'kidnapped four Commonwealth electoral officers from four different states, chopped them up, and redistributed them according to his own preferences.'

I grabbed the magazine from them and examined the pile of jeans closely. Relief, they weren't mine. The green splodge on the third pair from the top was a printing error, not green bubblegum.

'No more sudden moves,' shouted the kids. 'Your compulsively tidy wardrobe reveals you have serious criminal tendencies and we're taking you to the police.'

I started to walk out. 'This is preposterous nonsense,' I said.

The kids blocked my way. 'Come with us,' they said, 'or we'll put all your black shirts on white hangers.'

On the way to the police station I persuaded them to visit some of our neighbours so I could prove that tidy wardrobes are the norm in a civilised society and that rosters in the sock drawer do not necessarily lead to human heads in the freezer.

I was horrified by what I saw. Number 57's wardrobe was like something out of the Middle Ages. Wire hangers, shirts facing both ways and ties draped over the door handles. Number 59's was worse. Three garments to a hanger and not even matching fabric types. By the time the woman in number 61 sheepishly admitted she kept bras and panties in the same drawer, I didn't care about anything any more.

I stumbled into the police station hoping I'd get life so

that never again would I have to witness a chenille house-coat between two tweed jackets. Not unless the prison drama group did a modern-dress version of *Othello*.

The desk sergeant took my belt and shoelaces. Then he did something that restored my faith in humanity, civilisation and life itself. He put them into envelopes and wrote descriptions of them on the outside. Brilliant. When I get out of here I'm going to store all my accessories like that.

TRUST, LACK OF

'Where's the money?'
'Show me the suitcase first.'
1,853,267 crime movies

Is it any wonder we grow up with shrivelled trust glands?
From birth we're bombarded with the message that trust
is dangerous. Some of us absorb that message very early.
('OK, I'll suck the left one but I'm not sucking the other
'cause it poked me in the ear.) The rest of us move
warily through life, determined to keep our trust
alive in a dangerous and unpredictable world.
Then we start driving.

THE HUGE spine-crushing beast loomed over me and I
felt a quiver of fear run through my body, particularly
my spine. I tried to swallow. My mouth was dry. 'Are
we in any danger?' I squeaked.

'Nah,' said the salesman, 'the handbrake's on.' He

gave the huge bonnet a slap. The sound of quivering steel echoed around the showroom. 'Toughest four-wheel drive on the market,' said the salesman. 'Go on, kick a tyre.'

I hesitated.

'Go on,' said the salesman, 'it won't bite you.'

I gave a tyre a tremulous kick and jumped back. I wasn't worried about it biting me, I was worried about it slashing at me with its kerb-side mudguard and tearing my entrails out.

'Solid-steel chassis,' said the salesman, 'triple-reinforced bullbar, industrial-strength axles, loudest horn in its class and that kerb-side mudguard'll have a pedestrian's entrails out in less than a second. Only joking.'

I ran my eyes over the vehicle's mighty form and imagined how safe I'd feel in the supermarket car park sitting inside that much steel, atop that much rubber, next to that much plastic drink-holder. There was only one thing wrong.

'Um,' I said, 'have you got anything bigger?'

The salesman stared at me. 'Bigger?' he said. 'This is the biggest four-wheel drive on the market. Look at that bullbar. It takes the steel from seven crushed hatchbacks to make that bullbar. Why would you want anything bigger?'

'Well,' I said, 'it's like this. Remember how 15 years ago a few nervous and/or aggressive drivers started looking for larger, tougher vehicles and chose the four-wheel drive?'

The salesman went misty-eyed. 'Yeah,' he said.

'And remember how delighted those people were when

they discovered that the average family car just bounced off their new leviathans? And how average family-car drivers noticed it too, just before they blacked out? And how, as soon as they came out of traction, they rushed out and bought four-wheel drives themselves in such numbers that the four-wheel drive is now the average family car?'

'Yeah,' snuffled the salesman through tears of happiness.

'Well,' I said, 'I'm a nervous driver and I'm looking for a larger, tougher vehicle that the average family car will bounce off.'

The salesman looked confused. Then he gave me a scornful look. 'You've got to be joking,' he said. He stroked his product's 47-kilogram rear-view mirror. 'The only thing this'd bounce off is a semitrailer.'

'Were you looking for 16 wheels or 24?' asked the semi-trailer salesman.

I peered around the yard at the massive vehicles, unsure. 'Um,' I said, 'do you mean including the steering wheel and the spare?'

The salesman showed me a 24-wheeler rig with an engine the size of an oil refinery. I made a mental note to get the carport extended.

'What's your load?' he said. 'Ore? Livestock? Timber?'

'Kids mostly,' I said.

The salesman nodded. 'What sort of destinations?' he said. 'Across to Perth on the bitumen or up to Isa on the dirt?'

'Just down to the shops mostly,' I said. 'Plus the odd longer trip to the library.'

The salesman rolled his eyes, exasperated. 'Why didn't you say?' he exclaimed. He took me over to the biggest refrigerated truck I'd ever seen. 'This is more your style. Brilliant for getting the frozen pizzas home from the supermarket and the kids'll never complain about being hot in the back again.'

I gazed up at the massive bulk which was blocking out the sun and most of the sky. At last, a vehicle I could feel safe in, even in the school car park. I started signing the purchase forms. 'Does it have a light in the glovebox?' I asked.

'The number of people who ask that,' said the salesman. 'We sell a lot of these to women with kiddies. They usually go for the turbo diesel model with the tinted windows and the extra big bullbar.'

I stared at him, horrified. 'You mean other people are using these as family runabouts?'

The salesman looked surprised. 'Of course,' he said. 'Heaps. Mostly ex-four-wheel-drive owners who want something with a bit of extra grunt and a bit of extra space for carrying salvage if they hit something on the way to the video shop. They've gone for the semi 'cause it's the biggest, toughest vehicle you can get.' He laughed. 'You know, except for a tank.'

'Sorry, sir,' said the army transport disposal officer. 'We're clean out of tanks.'

'How about armoured troop carriers?' I ventured.

'Sorry,' said the officer. 'We had a group of women in this morning on their way to tennis.' His face brightened. 'I've got a four-wheel drive,' he said.

I shook my head.

He looked hurt. 'It's got a machine-gun,' he said.

As I drove home, my unusually small family car surrounded by four-wheel drives and refrigerated semis, I witnessed a remarkable thing. A young man with a tiny vehicle found himself in the path of a four-wheel drive that turned carelessly out of a driveway. For a horrible moment it looked as though he would perish on the bullbar. So low was his vehicle, however, that he passed underneath the brute steel without a scratch. Even as I blinked with astonishment, my brain was working overtime.

I wonder, I thought feverishly, if I could fit the whole family on a skateboard?

VANiTY

... every man therefore is but vanity.
Psalms

*Could it be – and don't finish reading this sentence if
you're easily worked up and/or you've just bought a
pile of expensive self-help books – that the whole human
self-help movement is based on vanity? Calm down, it's
just a question. I don't know if it is or not. This is my
fifty-sixth chapter intro and empty speculation's all
I've got left. One thing I do know. In a world where
judgements come at us from every direction, being
allowed a bit of vanity is only fair. OK, and puns.*

I SPENT two hours getting ready. First I had a shower, a
long hot one to cleanse my pores and leave my skin
looking its best and my pimples looking their best. Then
I shaved, twice, like all the men's magazines tell me I

should if I want to look really dapper. (They never give precise instructions for the second shave, so I just do my legs.)

Then I carefully blow-dried my hair, combed my eyebrows, trimmed my nasal tufts, smoothed on an exfoliating moisturising self-tanning lotion and cleaned my teeth with three different toothpastes. Where I was going I'd need a Macleans smile and a Colgate ring of confidence as well as a No Frills tongue.

Then I went into the bedroom to choose my wardrobe. After much deliberation, I settled on a white dinner jacket with a red bow tie and matching cummerbund, the whole ensemble set off by initialled cufflinks. (If I don't have one initialled 'L' and the other 'R', I can never tell which side they go on.)

'Wow!' said the kids. 'You look like a million dollars, plus GST. Where are you off to? Must be somewhere you need to look your immaculate best.'

'That's right,' I said. I'm going to the hardware store to buy some gutter clamps.'

The kids didn't believe me until they saw me loading a length of guttering into the car. 'We don't get it,' they said. 'Why go to all this trouble just for a shopping trip? Pierce Brosnan doesn't get this tarted up to make a movie.'

That's because, I reflected as I stopped at the traffic lights, Pierce only has to appear in front of one camera each day. If I had it that easy, I'd leave the hairs in my ears unplucked too.

I glanced up at the red-light camera pointing down at me from the corner of a nearby building and felt a surge of resentment. How dare we innocent citizens be subjected to uninvited televisual scrutiny like this? It was rude and intrusive, not to mention very inconvenient. I was sick of reversing up to traffic lights so the camera got my best side.

The other cars took even longer than usual to stop blowing their horns and let me turn round and as a result I was feeling a bit shaken as I drove on. So shaken, in fact, that I forgot to pause and wait for the sun to go behind a cloud before I went past the speed camera further down the road. As Pierce and his colleagues know, harsh sunlight does cruel things to the human face on camera, so I went back round the block for a retake.

Unfortunately, as I cruised past the camera again, I must have been looking at the sky rather than the speedo because I was booked. And the policeman rejected out of hand my offer to do a take three. Oh well, at least he was the same height as me so the two-shot of him pushing me over the bonnet of the car would have been nicely balanced.

At the shopping centre I parked as far away from the car park security camera as I could, as usual. The bloke who operates it hasn't got a clue. I've seen things on his cashier booth monitor that'd make you weep. Cars out of focus, sprinklers in shot, attempts to zoom and pan at the same time. Even first-year film school students and trainee car park attendants know you don't do that.

The red light on the camera in the lift was blinking so I adopted my usual stance, the one that minimises the light glaring off my bald patch, and thought nostalgically about the days when a lift provided a brief haven from the all-seeing eye of the lens. A place to adjust one's underwear. A place to suck one's teeth, particularly if one's underwear produces a lot of static electricity. My reverie was broken by a woman coming into the lift sucking her teeth. I tried to draw her attention to the camera, but it's hard giving effective hand signals when you're standing on your head.

I popped into the bank for some cash, and of course there were cameras everywhere. I've never been good in a multicam situation. At what point as you step from the queue to the teller are you moving into close-up? This is important to know if you've got a withdrawal slip in your mouth, a chequebook under your chin and a bank pen in your top pocket. And when you're chatting with the teller, does the bank cover that with a two-camera over-the-shoulder set-up or does the teller have to redo his lines later?

In the hardware store, reaching for the gutter clamps, trying hard not to get my cummerbund hooked on the paint-mixing machine, I saw it. The anti-shoplifting camera. This was the one I'd been dreading, partly because it's out of alignment and makes your face look green, and partly because sooner or later on camera my performance goes right over the top.

Which was exactly what happened. A few minutes later I placed my gutter clamps on the counter. Next to them I placed a lawnmower, 300 metres of cyclone fencing, a gross of assorted spanners, a chainsaw, six rolls of adhesive tar paper and a self-erect double garage.

I erected the garage in the shopping centre car park, got inside and wrote a letter to Pierce Brosnan.

Dear Pierce, I wrote, I can't stand the stress of being on camera any more. It's doing terrible things to my dress sense and my ego. Please help me get into the movies where at least I'll have a publicist to help me keep things in perspective. Ciao, Morris.

I haven't heard back. Pierce must have decided not to reply. He's probably too busy. Either that or there's a camera in his local post office.

WORRY

**Life is mostly froth and bubble,
Two things stand like stone,
Kindness in another's trouble,
Courage in your own.**
Adam Lindsay Gordon

*In the wee small hours, when I'm lying awake racked
with worry and I've forgotten everything I've ever read
in a self-help book, that simple verse often helps.
In particularly bleak moments I've tried to dismiss
it as platitudinous doggerel, but a few nights later there
it is again, soothing me. It even helped me through one
of the most worrying experiences of my life.*

I THOUGHT having a vasectomy was going to be torture.
You know, aaarrrggghhhhhh. It wasn't. It was more like
ooh ... aah ... eee ... aah ... ooh ... aah ... eee ...
aah ... ooh ... aah ... eee ... ahh ... ooh ... ahh ...
eee ... ahh. Though that was just the initial examination.

But I'm jumping ahead of myself. (Metaphorically

speaking. I won't actually be jumping ahead of myself for a couple of weeks. Not without pain-killers.)

It all started 11 months ago in the kitchen. 'You know what we've just had done to the cat,' I said to my partner. 'Well, I'm thinking of having that done to me.' My partner stared, mostly because what we'd just had done to the cat had involved a flea drench and a rectal thermometer.

'I mean last month,' I said. 'When we had the cat sterilised.'

My partner still looked surprised. 'The vet removed the cat's testicles,' she said. 'Are you sure that's what you've got in mind?'

I agreed it wasn't. My partner suggested I was probably thinking of a vasectomy. I checked in the dictionary to make sure a vasectomy involved absolutely no thermometers of any kind.

My partner gave me a warm and appreciative hug. 'This is wonderful,' she said, 'but it's also pretty permanent, so don't rush into it. Take your time. Think about it for a few days.'

I now wish I'd rushed into it. In the past I've never wanted to wait for anything involving even the slightest possibility of pain. My dentist is used to me ringing up to make an appointment from his waiting room.

This time, though, I took my partner's advice. I read medical books (OK, looked at the pictures). I made myself think about any remote and unlikely circumstances in which I might want more children (the government increasing child allowances, for example). I studied statistics on post-vasectomy depression and the incidence of rust on scalpels.

The process took more than a few days. Three hundred and twenty-six to be exact. But finally, a few weeks ago, I went to my GP for a referral. He was very thorough. He asked many searching questions, particularly about why I kept my legs crossed the whole time, including when I walked into his surgery.

I explained I was just a bit tense about having the op done too far from home. 'Call me a sook,' I said, 'but I need to know that if anything does go horribly wrong I'm not too far from a Band-aid and a chocolate frog.'

My GP understood. He referred me to a surgeon in a hospital only a short hobble from my place.

It was a wonderful hospital. Something about their modern, well-designed buildings and their stylish decor and their insistence on university-trained doctors made me feel relaxed as soon as I walked in.

I dropped to my knees and felt the quality of the carpet and knew I was in good hands. Which was strange, because I've often browsed in upmarket carpet shops and never felt the slightest inclination to let the salespeople cut open my testicles.

The surgeon was wonderful, too. He was actually a urologist, which I thought was very useful in case in the operating theatre I panicked and wet myself.

He was experienced, authoritative and very calm. His hands didn't even shake when I blew up a bag I found on his desk and crept up behind him and burst it. Or when he pointed out that it wasn't actually a bag, it was a replacement bladder for another patient.

So there I was, a man who for 40 years had successfully

avoided using the words 'testicle' and 'scalpel' in the same sentence, suddenly prostrate in a room full of people who'd all successfully combined both in the same career.

Normally I would have left. This time I couldn't because I was on my back with my genitals poking through a hole in a green sheet. A quick exit would not have been possible, I knew that from experience. (Canberra Amateur Dramatic Society, *Hair* auditions, 1972.) Plus it felt as if several of the people present were prodding and squeezing my rude bits. I couldn't be absolutely sure because another green sheet was being held up to block my view, possibly to protect the identity of the people involved.

It was very different from what I'd imagined having a vasectomy would be like. Blokes who reckoned they'd had one, but who I now suspect were confusing 'vasectomy' with 'vindaloo', had told me it would be quick, convenient and not particularly painful.

I'd imagined ducking into a family planning clinic where a friendly nurse would distract me with her views on John Howard's industrial relations policies, make a couple of quick incisions with the sharp end of a nail file and send me on my way. I hadn't expected an operating theatre with lights, cardiovascular monitoring equipment and enough support staff to divert the Snowy Mountains Hydro-Electric Scheme.

Having my private bits examined with the aid of 2,000-watt halogen spotlights would normally have been trauma enough in itself. (God knows it was on my honeymoon.) Suddenly it seemed a trifle compared to the increasingly close proximity of needle, scalpel and, as it turned out, razor. 'Just a quick shave,' said the surgeon.

I closed my eyes and prayed he was using something with a swivel head and a moisturising strip.

Next came the anaesthetic. 'Just a minor puncture,' said the anaesthetist, and my heart went out to him in gratitude because I knew how easily he could have said 'small prick'.

A blissful numbness started to creep over me, but it didn't creep very far. My brain, for example, remained unaffected. Which meant, as I heard the scalpel slice through my flesh, I was able to deduce that 'local anaesthetic' means 'anaesthetic that affects only a localised area' and not 'anaesthetic made in Australia'.

Soon I could smell cooking meat, and found myself pleasantly surprised that instead of the expected post-op sandwiches and tea, I'd be having a barbecue.

'Just cauterising the tube,' said a nurse. 'Weird, isn't it, the smell of your own flesh burning?'

I decided I'd probably give the post-op refreshments a miss.

'Just stitching you up,' said a voice, and my heart went out in gratitude that I was hearing this from a surgeon, not an investment adviser.

And that was it. One side done. Boy, I thought, I hope the other side's as quick, convenient and painless.

It wasn't. The problem, if my Latin translation is correct, was that the other tube, once it got wind that not only cutting but burning was imminent, took refuge somewhere extremely hard to get at. Either that or I'm deformed. I prefer to think the former, particularly as I've never unsuccessfully tried to leapfrog a bollard and have always worn a protector at cricket (even as a spectator).

Memo to manufacturer of local anaesthetic. Your

product is superbly effective with blade and heat-related pain. However, with the other sort of pain, the one that comes from having your testicle squeezed very hard, more work is needed. Urgently.

The nurses valiantly tried to distract me. They told me their views on John Howard's industrial relations policies. Basically, they want the entire Cabinet to have a vasectomy before the anaesthetic improves.

Eventually it was all finished and the surgeon asked me to point out, if I wrote about the experience, that for normal people with normal tubes a vasectomy would be much quicker, much more convenient and much less painful. Then he went off for vindaloo.

Scientists tell me it's impossible, other men with vasectomies claim it's never happened to them and the man in the fruit shop reckons I'm having delusions and should be eating more carrots.

Oh, how I wish they were right (except the bit about the carrots). But it is happening and in desperation I've decided to speak out.

It started several weeks after the op when I took a semen sample to the clinic. This is the final stage in the vasectomy process. You pay a pathology company an amount equal to a fuel pump in a Mercedes and they officially declare you to be a sterile organism.

A small dog was sitting outside the clinic. I bent down to pat it. Dogs have always adored me. I had a spine X-ray once, and apparently I've got a larger than average amount of marrowbone jelly.

But the dog outside the clinic didn't adore me. When I

reached down, it gave me a dismissive glance and walked away. I couldn't understand it. I didn't have any cat poo on my shoes. I wasn't wearing a dog suit in an over-obvious appeal for acceptance. I shrugged and decided the poor little mutt must have colic or a paranoid-psychotic personality disorder.

I wouldn't have given it another thought but for what happened a couple of hours later at my wood-chopping class. I've been learning wood-chopping for a few weeks now because a psychologist warned me that some men go a bit girly after vasectomies. Well, he's not actually a psychologist, but he reads a lot while his taxi's being serviced.

I chose wood-chopping because of its practical application. There's an old make-up table in my bedroom I want to get rid of, but it's too heavy for me to shift in one piece. Also, mark my words, wood-chopping will be a high-demand career skill in the new millennium despite the decline of agricultural shows. Once satellites carry all our communications and telegraph poles become redundant, there'll be big money for anyone who can shin up one and chop it into half-metre sections in less than four minutes.

But I digress. That's another thing that happens to men after vasectomies. They lose their powers of concentration. At least I think that's what happens. Somebody was telling me about it at length but I wasn't really listening.

So there I was, about to swing my mighty axe at a towering column of timber, when I saw a tiny face peering out of a knot-hole. It was a woodworm. It looked at me, looked at my razor-sharp blade, then turned its back on me and started eating. I couldn't believe it. After weeks of practice, just as I was very close to being able to swing the axe so it hit the wood, that creature assumed it could barge in and take over.

But my indignation soon turned to unease. Which increased when I got home and all my pets ignored me, except for a guinea pig who elbowed me aside as we both went for the same chair.

The horrible truth didn't dawn until I opened the fridge. My favourite cheese had mould on it. I was stunned. My longstanding deal with the micro-organisms in the kitchen that they could breed without hindrance everywhere except on my favourite cheese had broken down completely.

'Why?' I wailed. 'Why?'

'It's because you're sterile, Dad,' said the kids, looking up from their biology homework. 'The basic function of every organism is to reproduce. Lose that ability and you lose your cred in the natural world. As far as nature's concerned, you're surplus to requirements.'

I painfully digested the awful logic of their words.

'What about you?' I whispered finally. 'You're part of nature. Am I surplus to your requirements, too?'

They responded with big warm smiles. 'No, silly,' they said. 'You give us pocket money.'

That was some consolation, but only a bit.

Yesterday there was even worse news. My semen analysis has revealed a few stubborn sperm still present, presumably holding out for their super. I stared at the doctor's letter in horror. If nature's treating me this badly now, what's going to happen when I'm finally a sterile organism?

I've got to show nature I can still be useful. That's why as soon as I've finished this I'm going to check the pets for fleas and worms. I may no longer be able to reproduce, but I can still be a really good host for parasites.

AUTHOR'S NOTE

These pieces were first published, sometimes in slightly different form, in the *Good Weekend Magazine*, that fine publication which can be found tucked inside each Saturday's *Sydney Morning Herald* and Melbourne *Age*.

My warm gratitude to the *Good Weekend* editors and staff for their patience, help and unfailingly good-humoured approach to my punctuation.

Morris Gleitzman's books are moving, topical and hilarious. Here are some great reads for children from this award-winning and ever-popular writer.

Toad Rage

'Uncle Bart,' said Limpy. 'Why do humans hate us?'

Uncle Bart looked down at Limpy, and smiled fondly. 'Stack me, Limpy,' he chuckled, 'you are an idiot.'

Uncle Bart reckons humans don't hate cane toads, but Limpy knows they do. He's spotted the signs. The cross looks. The unkind comments. The way they squash cane toads with their cars.

Limpy is desperate to save his family from ending up as placemats. Somehow he must make humans see how nice cane toads really are. Risking everything, he sets off on a journey that is mucus-chillingly dangerous and wart-tinglingly daring. It's also very funny.

The epic story of a slightly squashed young cane toad's quest for the truth.

Gift of the Gab

I scribbled angrily in my notebook, ripped the page out and held it in front of his face.

'You killed my mother,' it said, 'and I've got the sausages to prove it.'

It starts off as a normal week for Rowena. A car full of stewed apples. A police cell. A desperate struggle to keep Dad off national TV.

Then her world turns upside down. And suddenly Ro is battling French policemen, high explosives and very unusual sausages to discover painful and joyous secrets that change her life for ever.

Bumface

Bumface!

That's who Angus wants to be. He dreams of being bold, brave, wild and free. Like the pirate in the stories he tells his younger brother and sister.

Instead Angus is just plain tired from changing nappies and wiping food off walls.

His mum calls him Mr Dependable, but Angus can barely cope. Another baby would be a disaster. So Angus comes up with a bold and brave plan to stop her getting pregnant.

That's when he meets Rindi.

And Angus thought *he* had problems . . .

The Other Facts of Life

Ben stared at the images on the TV screen half in fascination, half in horror.

He had never seen anything like this.

It was incredible.

It was awful.

He needed answers . . .

There are some things Ben doesn't understand, so his dad is sent in to explain the facts of life. But it's the other facts that are concerning Ben. His questions are pretty tough . . . and his dad just doesn't seem to have the answers.

But Ben is determined to make his point. He decides to find his own answers, and before long his inspired crusade even has the neighbours thinking he's a little weird. But he's not. He's deadly serious. And the result is very, very funny . . .

Second Childhood

'If you don't wake up to yourself, Smalley,' Mr Cruickshank
said, *'do you know what you're going to end up as?'*

'Sheep's poop, sir,' whispered Mark.

*Mr Cruickshank looked startled. 'I wouldn't have put it
quite like that.'*

Mark's father has always wanted him to be a Somebody.
But unless Mark picks up at school, it looks like sheep's
poop is where he's heading. Until Mark and his friends
discover they've lived before. Not only that – they were
Famous and Important People!

Wicked!

Morris Gleitzman and Paul Jennings
A NOVEL IN SIX PARTS
It'll suck you in.

Morris Gleitzman and Paul Jennings are Australia's most popular writers for children. Now they have written a book together. Twice as weird, twice as funny, twice as spooky, twice as mind-blowing. If you love their own books, you'll love *Wicked!* twice as much.

First published in six individual books, *Wicked!* was a runaway bestseller. Now available in a single volume, *Wicked!* is also being made into an animated TV series.

Winner of the 1997 KROC award and the
1998 COOL award (voted by children themselves)

In the Australian Publishers Association 1998 survey, Wicked! *1–6 was No. 1 in the Top Ten Children's Books, the Top Ten Australian Children's Books, the Top Ten Children's Fiction list and the Top Ten Australian Books list.*